Collins
Webster's

easy learning
GRAMMAR AND
PUNCTUATION

D0988542

HarperCollins Publishers
Westerhill Road
Bishopbriggs
Glasgow
G64 2QT

First edition 2011

Reprint 10 9 8 7 6 5 4 3 2 1 0

ISBN 978-0-00-736385-8

www.collinslanguage.com

A catalogue record for this book is
available from the British Library

Typeset by Davidson Publishing
Solutions, Glasgow

Printed in Great Britain by Clays Ltd,
St Ives plc

Editorial staff

American English consultant:
Orin Hargraves

Editor: Penny Hands

For the publisher:
Lucy Cooper
Kerry Ferguson
Elaine Higgleton
Lisa Sutherland

introduction

Collins Webster's Easy Learning Grammar and Punctuation is suitable for everyone studying English, and for students interested in the English language and how it works. The book gives clear explanations of the most important, frequent, and typical points of English grammar and punctuation, as well as providing the terminology needed to describe it.

The book begins with an outline of all parts of speech, and their structure and uses. All the main tenses of English are explained, with emphasis on their function in everyday English. Next, different types of sentence and clause are examined, with attention given to such structures as question forms, conditionals, and reported speech. Finally, a guide to punctuation gives students clear and up-to-date information on topics such as the apostrophe, capital letters, and the period.

Collins' focus on real English underpins our approach. The Collins Corpus is a 4 billion-word database of up-to-date English from thousands of spoken and written sources including everyday conversations, formal spoken English, newspapers, fiction, and blogs.

The corpus is at the heart of each grammar item, helping us make confident and accurate decisions about how English grammar works in today's world. Explanations are fully illustrated with examples that remain close to the corpus, occasionally with minor changes to avoid distracting or unhelpful elements.

Finally, we use our extensive experience in language teaching and learning to identify typical problems that students experience with the English language. Many of the most common errors have been noted and highlighted, with tips given to help learners avoid them. These include such issues as misuse of the apostrophe, overuse of exclamation points, and the mistaken use of important words.

We hope you will find *Collins Webster's Easy Learning Grammar and Punctuation* a valuable resource, both in the classroom and for personal reference.

Penny Hands, 2011

contents

contents

contents

Grammar

Parts of speech

Sentences are made up of **words**. A sentence can be made up of any number of words.

> *He left us.*
> *The man in the corner lowered his newspaper.*
> *Whenever I see Tammy I worry about how I look.*
> *Until tomorrow then.*
> *Yes.*

We can put words together in many ways to make new sentences.

> *I can help you.*
> *Can I help you?*

Grammar describes how we put words together. Each word in a sentence belongs to a particular set or **class**, depending on how it is used. These classes are called **parts of speech**.

All sentences begin with a capital letter and end in either a period, a question mark, or an exclamation point. When we talk about these marks, e.g., commas, semicolons, periods, parentheses, and so on, we are talking about **punctuation**.

The term **clause** is used to describe a group of words that contains a verb, the **subject** of that verb, and, often, some other words such as an **object**.

> *I live in Vermont.*
> *...where I live.*
> *Jessica lived in Memphis at first.*
> *He was living in Rome that year.*
> *...when he had eaten breakfast.*

A sentence can contain one or more **clauses**.

*I can help you **if you will let me**.*
***Whenever you need to talk to someone**, just drop in and see*
*   **if I'm here**.*

Many sentences are made up of a single clause. Single clause sentences are called **simple** sentences.

He arrived on Friday.
My brother loves his skateboard.

A clause always contains a **verb**.

run   *walk*
think   *believe*

A sentence, however, does not always have to be a clause. See p. 258 for more about clauses.

Certainly not.
Until tomorrow then.
Yes.
Why?

A **phrase** is just a **group** of words. The term is usually kept for words that go together naturally.

the other day
my friend Hank
in spite of
over the hill
would have been walking

Many words can refer to one thing only or to more than one. We use the terms **singular** and **plural** for this. A more general term is **number**. Pronouns and nouns can be singular or plural in grammatical number. See p. 200.

When we want to identify the speaker or the person spoken about in grammar, we use **first person** to mean the speaker, **second person** to mean the person who is spoken to, and **third person** to mean the person who is spoken about. For example, we talk about "first person plural" or "third person singular."

	singular	*plural*
1st person pronoun *2nd person pronoun* *3rd person pronoun*	*I* *you* *he, she, it*	*we* *you* *they*
nouns	*the man* *a girl*	*the men* *two girls*

A **verb** tells us about an action or a state of being. Ordinary verbs are called **main verbs**.

come	*go*	*think*
want	*economize*	*believe*

A special group of verbs are called **auxiliary verbs**. These can be put together with main verbs to form different tenses.

*I **am** thinking.*
*She **has** seen the movie already.*
*I **can** help you.*
*We **might** need to.*

A **noun** is a name for a thing or an idea.

table	*book*	*ugliness*
time	*animal*	*thing*

If we do not want to repeat the same noun in a sentence or a paragraph, we can replace it with a **pronoun**. A pronoun is a word that is used instead of a noun phrase or a noun.

> Gary saw Sue so *he* asked *her* to help him.
> Ross was hungry so *he* stopped at a coffee shop.

An **adjective** gives more information about a noun. Adjectives help us describe or pick out which particular thing among many is being referred to.

a man	*a **tall** man*
their TV	*their **new wide-screen** TV*
the cat	*the **fat black-and-white** cat*

A **determiner** is used to point more precisely to the person, thing, or idea that is being talked about. Examples of determiners are the **definite article**, the **indefinite articles**, and **possessives**.

the *cat*	*a man*
my *aunt*	***their*** *TV*

An **adverb** gives information about the way that an action is carried out or when and where it takes place.

> She ran **quickly** down the path.
> The children laughed **hysterically**.
> He lifted the box **carefully**.

Some adverbs can also be used before adjectives.

> He was a **rather** tall man.
> This cake is **quite** nice.
> It was **fairly** good.
> It's a **very** hot day.

Other adverbs can be used to introduce a sentence.

> **Fortunately**, *the rain stopped.*
> **Honestly**, *I can't help it.*

Many adverbs are formed from adjectives by adding -*ly*.

A **preposition** is one of a small group of words that can be used with nouns and verbs. Prepositions give information about position, movement, time, manner, and other things.

> **on** *the bridge*   **with** *a knife*
> **in** *the morning*   **to** *the gates*

When a preposition is used in front of a noun, the two together do the work of an adverb or an adjective.

> *He is coming* **now**.
> *He is coming* **in the morning**.
> *a* **rabid** *dog*
> *a dog* **with rabies**

A **conjunction** joins two or more nouns or clauses to each other.

> *I went to the store* **and** *bought some bread.*
> *I bought some bread,* **but** *I forgot to get milk.*

Many words can act as more than one part of speech. It is not unusual for an English word to be a **noun** in one sentence and a **verb** in another sentence.

> *Jamal scored several* **runs**.
> *She* **runs** *half a mile each morning.*
> *I've been chosen for the school* **play**.
> *Chris and Art* **play** *golf together on Fridays.*

Parts of the sentence

Sentences consist of a number of parts. The most important parts of a sentence are:

- The **subject**, which is either a noun phrase (see p. 133) or a pronoun (see p. 199). Normally the subject comes before the verb phrase in a sentence.

    The girls had been swimming.
    The new teacher came in.
    They had finished.

- The **verb phrase**, which includes the main verb and which may have auxiliary verbs to go with it. See also pp. 28–86.

    The girls had been swimming.
    The new teacher came in.
    They had finished.
    She uses her skateboard quite a bit.
    Rajiv was reading a new novel.
    She is riding someone else's horse.

- The **object**, which is a noun phrase or a pronoun.

    She used her old skateboard.
    Rajiv was reading a new novel.
    Josh found it.

Not all verbs need an object. When there is one, the object normally comes after the verb phrase. Some verbs may also need an **indirect object**. See also p. 227.

    Hamid gave me a party invitation.
    Ruth gave Lauren a nice bunch of flowers.

- An **adverbial**, or **adjunct**, which is an optional part of the sentence.

This may be:

– a single word, which will always be an **adverb**.

> *Suddenly, it started to rain heavily.*

– an **adverbial phrase**, which is a group of words that functions as an adverb.

> *In the morning, the sky was clear.*
> *You probably won't notice it after a while.*

– an **adverbial clause**, which is a group of words including a verb that functions as an adverb.

> *I'll get some cookies for you when I've poured the drinks.*
> *When I've poured the drinks, I'll get some cookies for you.*
> *Mark played while Mandy sang.*

Though some adverbials have a fixed position, most can be added to a sentence in several places.

> *In the winter, the roads get very slippery.*
> *The roads get very slippery in the winter.*

A sentence can have several different adverbials, some working together and some independent of each other.

● A **complement**. With certain verbs, such as *be* and *seem*, a complement takes the place of an object. A complement can be either an adjective or a noun phrase. Complements provide further descriptive detail about the subject. See also p. 229.

> *He became a doctor in 2005.*
> *Andrew is an auto mechanic.*
> *He felt a bit foolish when he realized what he'd done.*
> *They became good friends despite the mistake.*

Direct and indirect objects

The **object** of a sentence (if there is one) normally comes after the verb phrase. Whether there is an object or not depends on the meaning of the verb. For example, if you want to talk about what someone is doing, you might say "She is writing", but if you want to talk about the point of the activity, you might say, "*She is writing a book*."

> *She was riding.*
> *She was riding her horse.*
> *Erica was writing.*
> *Erica was writing a letter.*

An object that follows a verb like this is called the **direct object**.

> *Rory found a pen.*
> *Our cat doesn't like milk.*

Some verbs also have another sort of object, called an **indirect object**. An indirect object names the person for or to whom something is done. It is usually needed with verbs like *give*, *find*, and *owe*. For example, with *give*, we need to name both the thing that is given and the person (or sometimes, the animal) it is given to.

> *Mike owes Tom five dollars.*
> *Rob gave me a box of chocolates.*
> *Susan bought her rabbit some more food.*

Some verbs must always take a direct object, some never take a direct object; others sometimes take one and sometimes don't, depending on the meaning. When a verb has an object it is called a **transitive** verb.

> *Rowan bought a magazine.*
> *I don't like rap music.*

When it does not have an object it is called an **intransitive** verb.

>*Lynn fainted.*
>*Pavel screamed.*
>*Soon, everyone was shouting.*

Some verbs can be either **transitive** or **intransitive**.

>*Ann was reading (a letter).*
>*Kim was drawing (a picture).*

When a verb has both an indirect and a direct object it is called
a **ditransitive verb**.

>*Amy owes* **Mark** *ten dollars.*
>*Sarina gave* **me** *some flowers.*
>*Katie bought* **her hamster** *a new cage.*

A direct object is needed where the meaning of the verb requires
something to give it a focus. This is why we sometimes say that a direct
object "complements" a verb.

● Some verbs must have an adverbial as well as a direct object,
for example, to specify a place.

>*He placed* **the parcel** *on the chair.*
>*She put* **the umbrella** *in a corner.*

Verbs

Verbs are words that allow us to talk about activities, processes, states of being, and states of mind.

> This basket **holds** a lot.
> Josh **was reading** Kaitlin's essay.
> Frieda **is preparing** a talk for next week's class.
> Helen **feels** much happier now.
> I **forgot** that it **was** your birthday.
> Paul **owned** several old motorbikes.

Verbs can be divided into two major groups, according to the way they are used. Those in the larger group are called **main verbs**. The rest are called **auxiliary verbs**.

Verb phrase

A verb phrase can be a single word or a group of associated words.

> he **walks**
> he **is walking**
> he **had walked**
> he **can walk**
> he **has been walking**
> he **might have been walking**

When a verb phrase consists of a single word it is called a **simple** verb. Many verbs in English are made by combining an auxiliary verb and a main verb; this is called a **compound** verb.

- When we want to talk about all the parts of a verb, we use the term **verb phrase**.

Main verbs

Main verbs, or **lexical** verbs, are the verbs that we use to indicate actions and states. Most of the verbs in English are main verbs. Main verbs are divided or **classified** in several ways:

- according to whether they refer to **states**

    *I can really **taste** the herbs in this omelet.*
    *This scarf **belongs** to me.*
    *He **hates** losing.*
    *She always **liked** boats and sailing.*
    *I already **feel** that I **have known** you for ages.*

    or **actions**.

    *Three boys **were kicking** a ball around in the yard.*
    *We **were running** across the football field.*
    *For six hours, Stuart **drove** across open desert.*

- into **regular** and **irregular** verbs according to the spelling of their forms.

    regular: talk, talks, talking, talked
    irregular: swim, swims, swimming, swam, swum
    irregular: go, goes, going, went, gone

- according to whether or not they are followed by an object. That is, whether they are **transitive** or **intransitive**. See p. 80.

    *I can **read**.*
    *We both **read** **the same authors**.*
    *Don't **tell** **me**.*
    *We both **ran** away.*
    *Sue **found** **a bracelet**.*
    *I **saw** **my best friend** on Friday.*

Auxiliary verbs

These verbs are used in combination with main verbs in order to allow us to talk about different times or periods of time, different degrees of completion, and different amounts of certainty or doubt. There are several types of auxiliary verb. The primary auxiliaries help express time, and the modal auxiliaries help to express certainty and doubt. See pp. 35–74.

Tense

We use verbs to talk about actions and states. Verbs **tenses** allow us to talk about the time when the action or state takes place.

All main verbs have two simple tenses: the **present simple** and the **past simple**.

present simple	past simple
I walk	I walked
she sings	she sang
they come	they came
you bring	you brought

In these tenses the verb is used on its own without any auxiliary verbs.

English verbs also have compound tense forms. In these tenses the main verb is accompanied by one or both of the auxiliary verbs *be* and *have*. See p. 87 for more on tenses.

Aspect

The compound tenses of the verb express two **aspects**: **continuous** and **perfect**.

- The term **aspect** is used to talk about continuing actions versus completed actions or states. Simple tenses do not have aspect.

continuing actions	
I am walking	I was walking
she is singing	she was singing
they are coming	they were coming
you are bringing	you were bringing

completed actions	
I have walked	I had walked
she has sung	she had sung
they have come	they had come
you have brought	you had brought

We use these compound verbs when we want to talk about:

– the continuous nature of an action (using a form of the auxiliary *be* + *-ing*). This is called the **continuous aspect**.

> I *am* still **studying** French.
> He **was living** in LA all that year.
> Jamal **is helping out** with the children this week.
> Sarina and Scott **were looking** for a new apartment at the time.

– the completion of an action (using a form of the auxiliary *have* + a past participle). This is called the **perfect aspect**.

> I **have been** a teacher for four years.
> He **had lived** in Dallas for a year before coming to Denver.
> Jamal **has helped out** before.
> Sarina and Scott **had found** their apartment by then.

The two aspects of the verb can be joined so that we can talk about the duration and the completion of an action in the same verb phrase. See pp. 87–88 for more on tense and aspect.

> I **have been studying** French for four years.
> I **had been living** in Dallas for four years when I met him.
> Jamal **has been helping** us this week.

Simple tenses

Simple tenses show moments in time, timeless states, and habitual or repetitive actions.

> It **tastes** good.
> Julie **keeps** a diary.
> Adrian **went** home at midnight.
> She **heard** a strange noise in the night.
> Rob usually **walks** to school.
> Yesterday he **went** by car.

The **present simple** and the **past simple** of regular verbs are formed by using the base form of the verb. See pp. 93–97.

Continuous tenses

Continuous tenses show duration or continuity.

> It **is raining** hard this morning.
> It **was raining** when we came out of school yesterday.
> I'm **having** dinner. Can I call you back?
> He **was listening** to the radio when he heard the news.

The **present continuous** and the **past continuous** are formed from either the present or the past tense of the verb *be* + the **present participle** (or "*-ing* form") of the main verb. See pp. 98–101.

Perfect tenses

The present perfect tense can show that an action is completed but that it still has some importance in the present time. It can also show that a state began in the past and continues in the present.

> Ken **has walked** all the way from the station. (...and he's tired.)
> He **has** never **visited** me. (...and I'm feeling neglected.)
> She **has missed** the train. (That's why she's not here.)
> I **have lived** in Texas all my life. (I still live there.)
> My mother **has** always **believed** that I would succeed.
> (She still believes this.)

The **past perfect** is used to talk about something that happened in a time before a particular time in the past.

> He told us that he **had tried** it before.
> I **had** never **been** climbing before our activity holiday last year.
> She was late because she **had missed** her train.

The **present perfect** and the **past perfect** are formed using either the present or the past tense of the verb *have* + **the past participle** of the main verb. See pp. 102–105.

Perfect continuous tenses

Perfect continuous tenses show duration, completion, and importance in the present time or in the time referred to.

> I **have been working hard** in the garden all day.
> My mother **has been helping** me.
> My sisters **have been riding** this morning.
> I **had been working** in Italy that summer.
> Some of us **had been waiting** for two hours when the doctor appeared.

The **present perfect continuous** and the **past perfect continuous** are formed using either the present or past tense of the verb *have* + the **past participle** of *be* + the **present participle** of the main verb. See p. 106.

Other verb forms

Other verb combinations are used for positive or negative statements, or to express degrees of time and probability.

> *Do you **like** espresso coffee?*
> *I **don't like** fried food.*
> ***Could** I **have** a Coke, please?*
> *You **will be** in Atlanta within two hours.*
> *They **will** probably **meet** us at the airport.*

Types of main verb

Verbs of action

Most verbs describe an action such as *walking*, *running*, or *reading*.

> *John is **running** for the train.*
> *Haley **has** just **bought** a new camera.*
> *She **is putting on** an exhibition of her photographs.*
> *Ralph **has seen** the film already.*

- Action verbs can be expressed in all the tenses.

Verbs of state

Some verbs are used to talk about states of being or states of mind.

These include:

- verbs relating to the senses, e.g., *feel, hear, see, smell, taste.*
- verbs relating to emotions, e.g., *adore, fear, hate, like, love, want, wish.*
- verbs relating to mental activity, e.g., *agree, believe, expect, forget, mean.*
- verbs relating to possession, e.g., *belong, own, possess.*

> *I **feel** unhappy.*
> *I **hate** arguments.*
> *These flowers **smell** gorgeous.*
> *Raouf **wishes** he hadn't **agreed** to the plan.*
> *We **mean** you no harm.*
> *That car **belonged** to us once.*

- Verbs of state are not usually used in continuous tenses. When they are used in continuous tenses, they change their meaning.

> *I'm just **feeling** to see if the bone is broken.*
> *We **were tasting** some interesting New Zealand wines.*
> *Naomi **is expecting** a baby.*

There are some uses of the verb **be** that allow you to choose between a state or an action meaning. The word used as the complement makes an important difference.

> *Mark **is being** stubborn.*   **but not** *Mark is being tall.*
> *Oscar **is being** nasty.*   **but not** *Oscar is being intelligent.*

The verb **seem** has a limited number of adjectives that can be used as its complement.

> *Simon seems **happy**.*   **but not** *Simon seems tall.*

The forms of main verbs

English verbs have up to five different forms. These are:

1 the base form, e.g.,   *pull*
2 the 3rd person singular,
   present simple tense, e.g.,   *pulls*
3 the past simple tense, e.g.,   *pulled*
4 the past participle, e.g.,   *pulled*
5 the present participle, e.g.,   *pulling*

- Regular verbs are all formed in the same way, by building on the **base form** (form 1). This is the form you normally find in a dictionary. Most verbs are regular.

- Irregular verbs have different forms, particularly forms 3 and 4. See p. 32.

Form 1:   The **present simple** tense has all but one of its forms the same as the **base form**.

Form 2:   When the **present simple** tense has a 3rd person singular subject, the verb is formed from the **base form** + *-s*.

Form 3:   The **past simple** is formed from the **base form** + *-ed*.

Form 4:   The **past participle** is formed from the **base form** + *-ed*.

Form 5:   The **present participle** is formed from the **base form** + *-ing*.

A special variation of the base form is the *to* **infinitive**. There are a number of uses of a verb where both the words *to* + the **base form** must be present.

The base form is sometimes called the "bare infinitive."

As mentioned above, the 3rd person singular is formed from the **base form** + **-s**. Below are the exceptions to the rule:

Verbs ending in **-o**, **-ch**, **-sh**, **-ss**, **-x**, **-z**, or **-zz**: add **-es** to make the 3rd person singular, e.g.

veto	he veto**es**
catch	he catch**es**
focus	he focus**es**
push	he push**es**
miss	he miss**es**
box	he box**es**
buzz	it buzz**es**

Verbs ending in **-y** after a consonant:: change **y** to **i** and add **-es**, e.g.

carry	he carr**ies**
fly	he fl**ies**
worry	he worr**ies**

As mentioned above, the present participle is made up of the **base form** + **-ing**. There are some exceptions to the rule. Nearly all verbs that contain a short final vowel in front of a final consonant double the consonant before -ing, e.g.

sob	sobbing
bid	bidding
jog	jogging
run	running
stop	stopping
get	getting
put	putting

Irregular verbs

Irregular verbs are verbs that *do not* form the past simple tense and the past participle by adding -**ed** to the base form.

The three main groups of irregular verbs

In Group A, the base form, the past simple, and the past participle are the same:

1	the base form	*put*
2	the present simple tense	*puts*
3	the past simple tense	*put*
4	the present participle	*putting*
5	the past participle	*put*

A

bet	*cut*	*let*	*set*	*spread*
burst	*hit*	*put*	*shed*	*thrust*
cast	*hurt*	*shut*	*split*	*upset*

In Group B, the past simple and the past participle have the same form:

1	the base form	*buy*
2	the present simple tense	*buys*
3	the past simple tense	*bought*
4	the present participle	*buying*
5	the past participle	*bought*

B1

base form	past form	base form	past form
bend	bent	hang	hung
bind	bound	have	had
bleed	bled	hear	heard
bring	brought	keep	kept
build	built	kneel	knelt
buy	bought	lay	laid
catch	caught	make	made
find	found	say	said

Some of the verbs in Group B have alternative spellings for the past participle:

B2 The past form may be either *a* or *b*.

base form	past forms	
	a	*b*
burn	burned	burnt
dream	dreamed	dreamt
learn	learned	learnt
smell	smelled	smelt

The *a* forms are more common in American English.

In Group C, the base form, the past simple, and the past participle all have different forms:

1	the base form	*go*
2	the present simple tense	*goes*
3	the past simple tense	**went**
4	the present participle	*going*
5	the past participle	**gone**

C

base form	past forms		base form	past forms	
arise	arose	arisen	ring	rang	rung
awake	awoke	awoken	rise	rose	risen
bear	bore	borne	saw	sawed	sawn
begin	began	begun	see	saw	seen
bite	bit	bitten	shake	shook	shaken
blow	blew	blown	show	showed	shown
break	broke	broken	shrink	shrank	shrunk
fly	flew	flown	strive	strove	striven
give	gave	given	take	took	taken
know	knew	known	throw	threw	thrown
ride	rode	ridden	write	wrote	written

Auxiliary verbs

An auxiliary verb is a verb that is used together with a main verb to show time and continuity.

- *Be* and *have* are the **primary auxiliaries**. A primary auxiliary is used to construct compound tenses.

- *Be* is used to make present continuous and past continuous tenses.

    > I *am working*.
    > Randy *is using* the computer.
    > We *were* all *wondering* about that.
    > Kevin *was teaching* in Argentina in 1995.

    It is also used for the passive.

    > These books *are sold* in supermarkets.
    > Martin *was arrested* and held overnight.

See p. 40 for more on *be*.

- *Have* is used to make present perfect and past perfect tenses.

    > Aaron *has finished* fixing the car.
    > George and Alicia *have seen* the show already.
    > Amanda *had* already *eaten* when we arrived.
    > They *had* not *expected* to see us there.

See p. 44 for more on *have*.

- *Do* is the **supporting auxiliary**. It is used in forming negatives, questions, and emphatic statements.

    > *I do not like hot dogs at all.*
    > *Do you like shrimp?*
    > *You do like shrimp, don't you?*

See p. 48 for more on *do*.

See pp. 87–92 for more on simple and compound verb forms.

- *Will*, *may*, *might*, and the other verbs listed on pp. 53–54 are the **modal auxiliary verbs**, usually called, simply, **modal verbs** or **modals**. A modal verb allows us to talk about actions as possible, doubtful, or necessary.

    > *Charlie will go home on Friday.*
    > *Charlie may go home on Friday.*
    > *Charlie could go home on Friday.*
    > *Charlie must go home on Friday.*

Auxiliaries can be combined in a single verb phrase. For example, a verb phrase may consist of a **modal** + a form of *have* + a form of *be* + a form of a **main verb**.

    > *I could have been making a bad mistake by trusting him.*
    > *Sara will have been living in New Mexico for 2 years next month.*
    > *You must have been given the wrong number.*

The auxiliary verb, or if there is more than one of them, the first auxiliary verb, performs the following grammatical functions:

– it shows **tense** and is the **finite** part of the verb phrase.

    > *I have seen it.*
    > *She had seen it.*

She has been thinking.
She had been thinking.

- it shows **number** and **person** agreement with the subject.

  She has seen it.
  They have seen it.
  I am looking for it.
  You are looking for it.

- it will take any **negative** immediately after it.

  I do not want to do that.
  She has not been concentrating.

- it can come before the subject to make a **question**.

  Do you want to help us?
  Have you got a cell phone?

Contracted forms

Auxiliaries are very often used in contracted forms. In the case of *be* and *have*, the contracted form can involve linking the subject and the auxiliary verb into a single form, e.g. *I'm*, *I've*, *we'd* (*we had* or *we would*), *Sue's* (*Sue has* or *Sue is*).

  We're back!
  (We are back!)
  I've found it.
  (I have found it.)
  They'd gone when I got there.
  (They had gone when I got there.)
  Tom's here.
  (Tom is here.)

The contracted negative form **auxiliary** + *n't* is common with all the auxiliaries except *am*, e.g. *hasn't, wouldn't, don't*.

> She **isn't** *(is not)* trying.
> We **don't** *(do not)* live here.
> He **hasn't** *(has not)* seen it.
> I **can't** *(cannot)* come.

In standard English, the contracted form of ***am not***, when it is part of a question, is aren't.

> **Aren't** *I going to need some matches?*
> *I'm getting a ride with you,* **aren't** *I?*

● Contracted forms are more informal than full forms. They are
  therefore more common in spoken English. Full forms are usually
  preferred in formal written English.

Auxiliaries are used in sentence tags.

> *You had only had the carpet a week when the kitchen flooded,*
>   **hadn't you?**
> *It's Kaydance's birthday on Saturday,* **isn't it?**
> *You are joking,* **aren't you?**

See p. 241 for more about sentence tags.

Auxiliaries are also used to make a short addition to a statement,
such as:

– a positive addition to a positive statement, accompanied by *so*
  or *too*.

> *I went to the park and Latoya* **did too.**
> *I loved the movie, and* **so did** *Fred.*

– a negative addition to a negative statement, accompanied by *neither* or *nor*.

> *My dad never eats mussels and **neither do** I.*
> *I don't want to speak to Will now. – **Nor do** I.*
> *I can't understand it. – **Neither can** I.*

● Auxiliaries can be used in positive sentences to give emphasis. When they are emphatic they are never contracted.

> *You **have** made a mess!*
> *That **was** a nice surprise!*
> *I **am** proud of Kara. She's so clever.*

In the present simple tense and the past simple tenses the appropriate form of ***do*** is used to show emphasis.

> *I **do like** Pedro. – So do I.*
> *We **did have** a great time.*

An auxiliary on its own can be used to give a short answer to a question. Whatever auxiliary is used in the question is used on its own in the answer. The main verb is not repeated. Short answers are very common in spoken English.

> *Do you like avocados? Yes, I **do**. or No, I **don't**.*
> *Have you read anything by Michael Crichton?*
>   *Yes, I **have**.*

Be

The verb *be* is used as an auxiliary verb and it can also be used as a main verb. See p. 28.

The verb *be* is irregular. It has eight different forms: *be*, *am*, *is*, *are*, *was*, *were*, *being*, *been*. The present simple and past simple tenses make more changes than those of other verbs.

> I *am* late.   We *are* late.
> You *are* late.   You *are* late.
> He *is* late.   They *are* late.
>
> I *was* late.   We *were* late.
> You *were* late.   You *were* late.
> She *was* late.   They *were* late.

The present participle is *being*.

> He is *being* very helpful these days.

The past participle is *been*.

> We have *been* ready for an hour.

● The present simple tense forms of *be* are often contracted in normal speech. Note that the contracted form of *they are* is spelled *they're*, and not *their*, which is the possessive form of *they*.

> I'm here.   We're here.
> You're here.   You're here.
> He's here.   They're here.

Any form of *be* is made negative by adding *not* immediately after it. In speech, some forms of *be* also have contracted negative forms. Some of these forms emphasize the negative.

	emphasizes the negative
I'm not late. You aren't late. He isn't late. We aren't late. They aren't late. I wasn't late. You weren't late. He wasn't late. We weren't late. They weren't late.	You're not late. He's not late. We're not late. They're not late.

The major uses of *be* as an auxiliary verb are to form continuous tenses and the passive.

- **Continuous** tenses of main verbs use the appropriate form of *be*, present or past, followed by the present participle (or *-ing* form). See p. 98 and p. 106.

- The **passive** form of a main verb uses the appropriate form of *be* followed by the past participle. See p. 118.

The verb *be* is also used as a main verb. It is commonly found joining a subject to its complement.

As a **main verb**, *be* is used to talk about:

- Feelings and states. For this we use the simple tenses of the verb with a suitable adjective. See p. 87.

    I am delighted with the news but he is not happy.
    She was busy so she was not able to see me.

- People's behavior. For this we use the continuous tenses of the verb with a suitable adjective. See p. 96.

    *I **am not being** slow, I **am being** careful.*
    *You **were being** very rude to your sister when I came downstairs.*

- *Be* + the *to* **infinitive** is sometimes used to refer to future time. This is a somewhat formal use, which often appears in news reports. See pp. 128–132.

    *The President **is to visit** Japan in October.*
    *The Archbishop **is to have** talks with the Pope next month.*

- *It* + *be*: we use *it* as a subject when we are talking about time, distance, weather, or cost. In this use, *be* is always singular.

    *Hurry up, **it's eight thirty**!*
    *Is it? I didn't know **it was so late**.*

    ***It's** thirty miles to Great Falls from here.*
    *Come and visit us. **It's not very far**.*

    ***It's cold** today but **it isn't wet**.*

    ***It's very expensive** to live in Boston.*

- *There* + *is/are* is used to talk about something existing. In this use, the form that *be* takes may *be* singular or plural, depending on the number of the noun, and *be* is sometimes contracted.

    ***There's** a spare toothbrush in the medicine cabinet.*
    ***There was** a cold wind blowing.*
    ***There isn't** enough gas for the trip.*
    ***There are** several gas stations on the way, **aren't there**?*

To make the continuous tenses of the main verb *be* we have to use *be* twice, once as an auxiliary and once as a main verb.

>   You **are being** so annoying!
>   I know I **am being** childish, but I'm scared.

The question form of clauses with the verb *be* in them is made by putting the appropriate form of *be* right in front of the subject.

>   **Are you** better now?
>   **Is he** free this morning?
>   **Was he** cooking dinner when you arrived?

Have

The verb *have* is used as an auxiliary verb –

> She *has* finished writing her dissertation.
> Karl *had* read about the concert in the newspaper.

and also as a main verb. See p. 24.

> She is *having* a massage at the moment.
> The driver has *had* his breakfast, so we can go.

The verb *have* has these forms: *have*, *has*, *having*, *had*. The base form of the verb is *have*. The present participle is *having*. The past tense and past participle form is *had*.

- The present and past forms are often contracted in speech, especially when *have* is being used as an auxiliary verb.

  The contracted forms are:

have = **'ve**	I*'ve* seen the governor.
has = **'s**	He*'s* gone on vacation.
	Jan*'s* behaved badly.
had = **'d**	You*'d* better go home.
	Jake*'d* left them behind.

The form *have* contracts to *'ve*. This can sound rather like *of*, especially after other auxiliary verbs.

> She **would've** given you something to eat.
> You **could've** stayed the night with us.
> If he'd asked, I **might've** lent him my car.

Avoid the common mistake of writing *of* in sentences like the ones above.

As an **auxiliary** verb, *have* is used to make the **perfect tenses** of main verbs.

The **perfect** tenses of main verbs use the appropriate form of *have*, present or past, followed by the past participle. See pp. 102–109.

> I **have read** *some really good books over the holidays.*
> I **had seen** *that episode before.*

The negative of a clause containing a compound verb with *have* is made by adding *not* or another negative word immediately after the appropriate form of *have*. In speech, some forms of *have* also have contracted negative forms.

> I **have never seen** *such luxury.*
> *Rachel* **had not been** *overseas before.*
> *She* **had hardly had** *time to eat when Paul arrived.*

- Present tense and past tense forms that emphasize the negative element:

  I/we/you/they'**ve not**;   *he/she/it*'**s not**
  I/we/you/he/she/it /they'**d not**

  > *She*'**s not** *told me about it yet.*
  > *We*'**ve not** *been here before.*
  > *They*'**d not** *seen him for weeks.*

- Present tense and past tense negative forms that are used less emphatically:

  I/we/you/they **haven't**;   *he/she/it* **hasn't**
  I/we/you/he/she/it /they **hadn't**

  > *He* **hasn't** *found anywhere to stay on this trip.*
  > *We* **haven't** *been here before.*
  > *They* **hadn't** *looked very hard, in my opinion.*

As a **main verb**, *have* is used to talk about:

● states or conditions, such as possession or relationship.

– In these senses, continuous tenses are not used in standard English. With this meaning *have* is sometimes used alone, adding only *not* to make negatives, and adding nothing to make questions.

> *I **have** something for you.*
> ***We haven't** any reason not to attend.*
> ***Have you** no sense of shame?*
> *The driver **has had** his breakfast, so we can go.*
> *We **had** a good time.*

It is also often used with forms of *do* to make negatives and questions.

> ***Do you have** a pen?*
> ***Does she have** my umbrella?*
> ***She doesn't have** any brothers or sisters.*
> ***Do you have** time to see me now?*

● **Have got** is an informal form of this main verb use of *have*, often used in speaking.

> *I **haven't got** any brothers or sisters.*
> ***Has she got** my umbrella? – Yes, she has.*
> ***She hasn't got** any money.*

Notice that the participle is *got*, not *gotten* for this meaning (i.e, to show possession).

● activities, including those such as eating, and leisure.

This meaning of *have* sometimes uses continuous tenses. For simple tenses, negatives and questions are formed using one of the forms of *do*.

> *He was having* a seizure when I phoned.
> I'm *having* lunch at twelve o'clock.
> Come and *have* a sandwich with me,
> No thanks. I *don't* usually *have* lunch.
> He's *having* a difficult day.
> *Did* you *have* a good vacation?

Contractions and weak forms are not possible with this meaning. *Have got* is also not used with this meaning.

- to express obligation or necessity using *have to* or *have got to*.

> I've *got to* go now, I'm afraid.
> *Do* you *have to* leave so soon?
> *Have* you *got to* leave so soon?
> The package *has to* go out today.
> The package *has got to* go out today.

When *have* is a main verb, it makes perfect forms like all other main verbs. This means that it is possible to use *have* twice in present or past perfect sentences, once as an auxiliary verb and once as a main verb.

> We *have had* enough, thank you.
> They *had* already *had* several warnings.

Do

The verb *do* is used as an auxiliary verb.

I **do** not want it.	We **do** not want it.
You **do** not want it.	You **do** not want it.
He **does** not want it.	They **do** not want it.

I **did** not want it.	We **did** not want it.
You **did** not want it.	You **did** not want it.
She **did** not want it.	They **did** not want it.

Do can also be used as a main verb. See p. 28. When *do* is used as an auxiliary verb it is a **supporting verb**. Because a main verb cannot combine directly with negatives or make questions, *do* is used to support the main verb.

> **Don't** talk!
> **Don't** run!

It is also used to stand in for another verb to avoid repetition, as shown on p. 39.

The verb *do* is irregular. It has five different forms: *do*, *does*, *doing*, *did*, *done*. The base form of the verb is *do*. The past simple form, *did*, is the same for all persons, singular and plural. The present participle is *doing*. The past participle is *done*.

The present simple tense *do* and the past simple tense *did* can be used as an auxiliary verb. As an auxiliary, *do* is not used with **modal** verbs.

I **do** not want it.	We **do** not want it.
You **do** not want it.	You **do** not want it.
He **does** not want it.	They **do** not want it.

I *did* not want it.	We *did* not want it.
You *did* not want it.	You *did* not want it.
She *did* not want it.	They *did* not want it.

As an **auxiliary** verb *do* is used in the following ways:

– to help make the negative and question forms of present simple and past simple tenses.

> Oh dear, I **didn't feed** the cat this morning.
> **Do** you **know** what time it is?
> **Did** Tim **pay** for his ticket last night?

– to make the negative form of a command.

> **Don't** talk!
> **Don't** run!

– to make a command more persuasive. See p. 245.

> **Do** let me see it!

– to avoid repeating a main verb in additions, commands, sentence tags, and short answers.

> They go to the movies often, **and so do** we.

> Don't run on the road! Don't **do** it!

> You live in Sioux Falls, **don't** you?

> Do you play baseball? – No, I **don't**.
> Did they tell you the news? – Yes, they **did**.
> Jim likes jazz, I think. Yes, **he does**.

– in comparisons when the verb in the first clause is in a simple tense.

> *She **sings** better than I **do**.*

The positive forms of *do* cannot be contracted. In speech, the negative has contracted forms.

> *I **don't** (do not) agree with you.*
> *She **doesn't** (does not) live here now.*
> *They **didn't** (did not) buy any food.*

- Present tense negative forms:
  I/we/you/they **don't**; he/she/it **doesn't**

- Past tense negative form:
  I/we/you/he/she/it/they **didn't**

When *do* is a main verb, it has a range of meanings that includes *carry out*, *perform*, *deal with*, or *provide*. It is sometimes used in place of a more specific verb.

> *I'll **do** the lawn now.*
> *(I'll **mow** the lawn now.)*
> *I'll **do** your hair.*
> *(I'll **arrange** your hair.)*
> *We don't **do** wedding receptions.*
> *(We don't **provide** wedding receptions.)*

It is then used with the full range of tenses and forms. See also p. 93.

> *Are you **doing** your homework?*
> *You **have been doing** well this semester.*
> *She **had done** enough, so she stopped.*
> *This **has been done** before.*

The main verb use of *do* can be used to talk about:

– habits.

> I *do* the dishes every evening.
> This is what I usually *do*.

– behavior.

> He *did* something pretty stupid.
> I *didn't do* anything wrong.
> What *are* you *doing*?

– plans.

> What *are* you *doing* on Sunday?

As a main verb, *do* makes negatives and questions like all other main verbs:

– in the present simple tense with auxiliary *do*.

> What *does* he *do* for a living?
> *Do* I *do* it this way?
> No, you *don't do* it like that at all.

– in the past simple tense with auxiliary *did*.

> *Did* Hank *do* it, then?
> *Didn't* Hank *do* it, then?
> He *didn't do* it, you know.

This means that it is possible to use *do* twice in negative and interrogative sentences; once as an auxiliary verb and once as a main verb.

- As a main verb, *do* can be used with modal verbs.

    *They **will do** it for you, if you ask nicely.*
    *I **can do** it, but I **shouldn't do** it.*

Modal verbs

Modal verbs are a particular kind of **auxiliary**.

> *Look, I can do it! – Oh yes! So you can.*
> *Can I use your phone? – Of course you can.*
> *Do you think she will come? – I'm sure she will.*
> *I must get our tickets today.*

Modal verbs are used when you need to add special elements of meaning to a main verb, e.g.:

– to express different degrees of doubt and possibility about the action of the main verb.

> *I may not be able to do it.*
> *I think that I might have caught your cold.*
> *I could ask for you, if you like.*
> *You couldn't do it, could you?*

– to express degrees of future possibility, ranging from the definite future, *will*, to the possible future, *may*, and the conditional future, *could*.

> *You will be seeing her on Friday at Jackie's house.*
> *I may be late coming home tomorrow evening.*
> *I could bring some more bread home with me tonight.*

– to request or give permission for an action to take place.

> *May I come in?*
> *You can borrow my car tonight if you like.*

– to prohibit or discourage something, when used with a negative.

> *You shouldn't use this computer without permission.*
> *You cannot borrow my car tonight.*
> *He must not see this letter.*

– to speculate.

> *The weather's so bad the flight **could** be late.*
> *It **might** be all over by the time we get there.*
> *He **may** be really angry about all this.*

– to express obligation, necessity, or duty.

> *I **must** turn in my essay today.*
> *The clutch **must** be disengaged to start the engine.*
> *Helen **ought to** tell the truth.*

– to refer to typical behavior.

> *She **can** be very helpful on occasions like this.*

– to add politeness to a request that might otherwise sound abrupt.

> ***Would you** please close the door?*

– to make conditional sentences (see p. 272).

– in reported speech (see p. 278).

Modals can refer to a time range that reaches from the immediate present to some future time, so that they can all be used for future reference, especially when they are used with a time adverbial. See pp. 110–117.

> *You **will be seeing** her **on Friday** at Jackie's house.*
> *I **may** be late coming home **tomorrow evening**.*
> *I **could** bring some more bread home with me **tonight**.*

Some modals can refer to a time range that goes back from the immediate present to some indefinite past time. They can refer to habitual action when they are used with a time adverbial.

> *When I was little, I **would** ride my bike around and around the lawn.*

Form

Unlike other verbs, modal verbs have only one form, the **base form**, and only one tense, the present simple.

> You **will** be seeing her **on Friday** at Jackie's house.
> I **may** be late home **tomorrow evening**.
> I **might** go to visit Grandma **on Saturday**.

They do not have a **to** infinitive. They have no -s inflection in the 3rd person singular.

> **He will** be seeing her on Friday.
> **She may** be late coming home.

- Since modal verbs do not have past tense forms, you have to use other verbs to provide some of the modal meanings in the past. For example, past necessity is expressed by **had to** instead of **must**.

> I **must** visit Aunt May today.
> I **had to** visit Aunt May yesterday.

- The modals **shall** and **will** are usually contracted to **'ll** in spoken English. All the negative forms can be contracted to form a single word such as **can't**, **won't**, **wouldn't**. These contracted forms are common in both spoken and written English.

> I will/shall = **I'll**
> We will/shall = **we'll**
> You **mustn't** say things like that, Jane.
> John **can't** come to my party.

There are other contracted forms such as **he'll**, **we'll**, and **they'll**, that are common in spoken English but less common in written English.

- Several verbs act as modals sometimes and as full main verbs at other times. These are called **semimodal verbs**. Their forms vary depending on whether they are used modally or as a main verb.

  *How **dare** he!*
  *He **dared** to ask me to do his laundry!*
  *She **need**n't come if that's how she feels.*
  *Monica **needs** a new raincoat.*

Position

Modals come before any other auxiliary verb or main verb in the verb phrase.

- Modal verbs are followed by the **base form** of the verb if there is no other auxiliary verb present.

  *Yes, you **can borrow** those earrings tonight.*
  *You **should try** that new restaurant in town.*
  *You **must come** over again some time.*

If one of the auxiliary verbs *have* or *be* follows the modal verb, the main verb will take the appropriate present or past participle form.

  *I **may have upset** him.*
  *You **could have looked** for it yourself.*
  *Janice **might be coming** too.*
  *Sunita **will have been worried** about her, I imagine.*

- In negative sentences, *not* comes immediately after the modal verb and in front of all the other verbs.

  *They **may not wait** for you if you're late.*
  *He **must not be** disturbed after 9 o'clock.*

- *Can* cannot be combined with the auxiliary form *have*, but the negative form *can't* can be combined with *have*.

    They can't have seen him.   **but not** *They can have seen him*

Can and could

Both these verbs indicate ability in some respect. The use of *could* is usual in clauses that contain a reference to past time, and in these cases it may be helpful to think of *could* as the past form of *can*.

> *Morry can speak French quite well now.*
> *I couldn't play chess two years ago, but I can now.*
>
> *When I was younger I could play tennis really well.*
> *Winston is so strong he can lift me right off my feet.*
> *Can you get up the stairs without help?*
> *You can come over for dinner whenever you like.*

Can and *could* are used:

– to indicate that you know how to do something.

> *Mary can solve these equations.*
> *I couldn't draw very well when I was younger.*

– to show ability to do something. (Compared with *be able to*, *can* indicates ability in a more general way that includes "is allowed to.")

> *When I was younger I could ski really well.*
> *Greg can run ten miles in 25 minutes.*
> *Are you able to walk to the car?*

– to make polite requests or to ask for permission:

Could is more tentative than *can*. (Compare with *may*, which is more formal.)

> *Can I borrow the car tomorrow evening, Mom?*
> *Could I come with you on the trip?*
> *May I take this book home with me?*

– to express the possibility of an action in the future, especially when the possibility is related to plans or projects. (Compare with *may*, where the possibility referred to is still uncertain and in the future.)

> We *can* go to Paris next week since you are free.
> We *could* go to Paris next week if you are free.
> We *may* go to Paris, but it depends on our finances.

– to express the possibility of an action in the present.

> You *can* dive off these rocks; it is safe here.
> We *could* dive off the rocks, but we have to be careful.

– to talk about actions that were possible but did not happen, using *could* + the perfect form of *have*.

> Mariel *could have stopped* the fight but she didn't.

– using the perfect form of *have*, to speculate about actions that have recently taken place.

> Who *could/can have broken* the window?
> Who *would have guessed* that they were related?

A distinction between *can* and *could* is observed in conditionals. *Could* is used when the conditions are not met.

> If Louisa is coming, she *can* look after the children for a while.
> If Helen had more money, she *could* buy a computer.

When changing sentences from direct to reported speech *can* is usually changed to *could*.

> Bernard said, "I *can* do it for you, Stu."
> Bernard said that he *could* do it for Stu.

---

can
The negative form is: *cannot*.

>   I *cannot* understand why he did it.

The contracted negative form is: *can't*.

>   I *can't* help it.

could
The contracted negative form is: *couldn't*.

>   I *couldn't* help it.

May and might

Both *may* and *might* can be used in requests and in expressions of possibility for the present and future.

> *Might I ask you your name?*

> *The weather **may/might** be better tomorrow.*
> *Craig **may/might** know his results soon.*
> *We **may/might** go to the movies tonight.*
> *"**May** I come with you?" Nicky asked.*

May and *might* are used as follows:

− *May* is used to ask permission in a more formal way than *can*.

> ***May** I have a drink, please?*
> ***May** I use your ruler? I've lost mine.*

Might is occasionally used in formal situations.

> ***Might** I suggest a different solution?*

− *May* is used to give permission, particularly when applied to *you*, *he*, *she*, *they* or a proper noun, to show that the speaker is allowing something to happen.

> *You **may** go now.*
> *Users **may** download forms from this website.*

− Both *may* and *might* are used to express the possibility of some future action; *might* is less certain than *may*.

> *The weather **may/might** be better tomorrow.*
> *Craig **may/might** know his results soon.*
> *We **may/might** go to the movies tonight.*

– *May* is often used for politeness, to make an order appear as a request; *might* is used to make the speaker less personally involved with the request.

> *You **might** give that idea a bit more consideration.*
> *You **might** want to move a bit closer to the screen.*

– *Might* is occasionally used when someone is trying to persuade another person to do something, perhaps with some degree of irritation. This use is a little old-fashioned.

> *You **might** give me some cake too, Luke.*
> *Anna, come on, you **might** tell me what he said!*

● When *might* is used in a conditional sentence, the *if* clause can be in the present or the past tense. Compare with *could*. See p. 58.

> *If Lakesha **comes**, she **might** look after the children.*
> *If Lakesha **came**, she **might** look after the children.*

When changing sentences from direct to reported speech may usually becomes *could*.

> *"**May** I come with you?" Nicky asked.*
> *Nicky asked if she **could** come with them.*

may
The contracted negative form is:　　*mayn't*

(Archaic only; not used in contemporary American English).

might
The contracted negative form is:　　*mightn't*.

> *It **mightn't** be so hard to explain.*
> ***Mightn't** there be a better way to do this?*

Must

Must is used to express obligation and necessity, and to give orders in a formal way. It can only be used for present and future reference. When the past is involved, you use *have to*.

Must is used:

– to express obligation.

> *All students **must** bring a packed lunch tomorrow.*

– to express necessity.

> *The key **must** be inserted before you press the switch.*

– to give orders firmly.

> *You **must** go to sleep now.*

– to speculate about the truth of something.

> *She **must** be mad!*
> *You **must** be joking!*
> *There **must** be some mistake.*
> *Mr. Robertson is here; it **must** be Tuesday.*

When this sort of statement is made in the negative or interrogative, *can* is used instead.

> *Can Mary be joking? **Can** she really mean that?*
> *You **can't** be serious!*
> *It **can't** be true!*

- *Must* can be used in the interrogative, but many speakers use *have to* instead.

    > *Must you* go so soon?
    > *Must I* invite Helen?
    > *Do you have to* go soon?
    > *Do I have to* invite Helen?

You can use *must* with a negative:

- to forbid someone to do something.

    > You *must not* cross when the light is red.
    > Passengers *must not* leave baggage unattended.

- to talk about an event or state that is unacceptable.

    > There *mustn't* be any mistakes in your letter.
    > The whale *must not* become extinct.

> Note that to express the fact that you are not obligated to do something, you use *do not have to*.
>
> Compare:
>
> > You *must not* come in here (you are forbidden).
> > You *don't have to* come in here (if you don't want to).

- It is necessary to change *must* to *have to* when changing sentences from direct to reported speech.

    > "I *must* fill out those forms this evening," said Janos.
    > Janos said that he *had to* fill out some forms.

must
The contracted negative form is: *mustn't*.

> You **mustn't** worry so much.

Shall and will

The normal way to express simple future time in English is using the modal verb *will* followed by the **base form** of a main verb.

> The modal verb *shall* is not used very much in modern spoken English, except in suggestions or offers of help.
>
> *Shall I help you?*
> *Shall I cook supper?*
> *Shall we go to the movies tonight?*

A distinction between *will* and *shall* is difficult to make in spoken English, since the contracted form, *'ll*, is used to mean both *shall* and *will*.

Shall is used:

– with questions involving *I* and *we* when the speaker is making a suggestion or offering help.

> *Shall I help you?*
> *Shall I cook supper?*
> *Shall we go to the movies tonight?*

– in many legal and formal contexts where authority is implied or where there is a legal obligation.

> **All visitors** *shall leave the park by 9 p.m.*
> **Both parties** *shall give three days' notice of any change in terms.*

Because *shall* was used frequently in earlier times, it still appears in many older texts that people memorize, such as poems, hymns, and nursery rhymes.

Will is used:

– with *I* and *we* to show intentions and to make promises.

> *Don't worry. I **won't** be late.*
> *We **will** be in touch.*
> *I **will** try to ensure that you get a good room.*

– with *you, he, she, it,* and *they,* to give reassurances.

> *Helen **won't** be late.*
> *He **will** be well treated.*
> *You **will** have your money next week.*

– to insist on something. Full forms are normally used, and are stressed in speech.

> *You **will** do what I tell you!*
> *Janet **will** go to Mary's even if I have to carry her there.*

– to make polite requests and to give invitations.

> ***Will** you help me look for my purse?*
> ***Will** you come to lunch on Friday?*

– to give orders.

> *You **will** finish your work before you watch TV, **won't** you?*
> *Luke, **will** you please be quiet!*

– to show prediction.

> *The match **will** be finished by now.*
> *I think it **will** probably rain tomorrow.*

– to show that someone persists in doing something. This use requires the full form with stress and is somewhat literary or old-fashioned.

> *Oh! Tony **will** keep bumping me when I'm trying to write!*
> *No wonder you feel sick. You **will** eat chocolate all day long.*

will
The contracted form is: **'ll**.

> *He'll be home soon.*

The contracted negative form is: **won't**.

> *Eve **won't** speak to Harriet.*

shall
The contracted form is: **'ll**.

The contracted negative form is: **shan't**

> *I **shan't** say a word.*

(Used mainly in British English; extremely rare in American English.)

Should

The modal verb *should* is used in the following ways:

– to talk about moral obligation. Compare *ought to* on p. 73.

> They *should* do what you suggest.
> People *should* report this sort of thing to the police.
> She suggested we *should* visit Irene more often.
> Rob insisted that we *should* think of others before ourselves.

– to give advice or instructions.

> You *should* undo the top screws first.
> You *should* keep your credit card separate from your checkbook.

– to suggest that something is probably true, though you have no way of knowing for sure.

> They left here at 6 o'clock, so they *should* be home now.
> The cherries *should* be in bloom when we arrive.

– to show politeness in a conditional clause. This use occurs in formal written communication.

> If you *should* decide to go, please contact us.
> *Should* you need more information, please call the manager.

● *Should* can be used with the main verb after certain set expressions such as *it is a pity that*, *it is odd that*, *I am sorry/surprised that*. This is a more formal use than the same expression without *should*, or than the same expression with *would*.

> It's a pity that this *should* happen.
> I was quite surprised that he *should* be doing a job like that.

- *Should* + the perfect form of the main verb can be used to express regret about something that was done or not done. Compare with *ought to*.

  > He **should have stopped** at the red light.
  > You **should have told** me you were ill.

- When changing sentences from direct to reported speech, *should* does not change.

  > Anna said that I **should** try to relax more.

In British English, *should* is sometimes used with *I* or *we* in conditional clauses, instead of the more common *would*.

  > I **should** love to visit Peru **if I had the money**.
  > We **should** hate to miss the play.

In this sense, *would* is more common in modern spoken English and the only form used in American English.

  > I **would** love to visit Peru.
  > We **would** hate to miss the play.

should
The contracted negative form is: ***shouldn't***.

Would

The modal verb *would* is commonly used as follows:

– to make a polite request.

> *Would you mind moving your bag?*
> *Would you give me a hand with this ladder, please?*

– to offer something politely.

> *Would you like some tea or coffee?*

– together with *like* as a polite form of *want*.

> *We would like to see Mr. Brown now, please.*
> *My friends would like to see your garden.*

– to refer to habitual activity in the past, with the meaning of *used to*.

> *I remember Jeff; he would watch TV all day if you let him.*
> *Jessica was a kind girl; she would always go out of her way to help people.*

– to show that someone persisted in an activity in the past: **would** is sometimes stressed here.

> *John would keep nagging at her, though I asked him not to.*
> *She would go on and on until I lost my temper.*

– to express and ask about probability.

> *I saw a girl at the window. Who would that be?*
> *Oh, that would be his elder sister!*

– in conditional clauses, usually together with an **if** clause.

> I **would** have taken it if it had been available.
> If you offered me some more I **wouldn't** refuse.
> Brian **would** have phoned the police if it he'd seen the accident.

When changing sentences from direct speech to reported speech, **will** is usually changed to **would**.

> Anna said, "Raymond **will** help you."
> Anna said that Raymond **would** help us.
> James said, "The car **won't** start!"
> James said that the car **wouldn't** start.

would
The contracted form is: **'d**.

> I**'d** have done it too, given the chance.
> We**'d** like to look at the garden.
> He**'d** be very angry if he knew about it.

The contracted negative form is: **wouldn't**.

> Even if he'd known about it, he **wouldn't** have been angry.

Ought to

The use of *ought to* is similar to *should*, but it is not used as widely. It is usually more informal than should.

Like *should*, the verb *ought to* does not have a past form.

Ought to isn't typically used in questions and negatives, but there are some exceptions in formal and very informal language.

In negatives, *not* comes between *ought* and *to*. In questions, the subject comes between *ought* and *to*. This use is formal.

> I **ought not to** have said those things to her.
> **Ought** we **to** make such a sacrifice for the benefit of future generations?

The negative form *oughtn't* is used by some speakers; it is considered informal. When *oughtn't* is used, it does not always require *to* before the infinitive.

> I **oughtn't to** have said those things to her.
> You **oughtn't** be so friendly to strangers.
> **Oughtn't** we call first to see if they're open?

Ought to is used as follows:

– to express an obligation or an expectation that someone should do something.

> You **ought to** listen carefully.
> We **ought to** leave now.
> Linda **ought to** go by herself.
> People **ought to** be a bit nicer to us.

- to express the likelihood of something happening.

    *Anup **ought to** be here by now.*
    *The journey **ought to** take about 2 hours.*

- *Ought to* + *have* + **past participle of main verb** is used to express regret that something was not done or to reproach someone for doing or not doing something.

    *I **ought to have spoken up** earlier. I'm sorry.*
    *You **ought to have offered** to help.*
    *They **oughtn't to have told** us everything was taken care of.*

● In questions and negatives, *should* is frequently used instead of *ought to* because it sounds more natural.

    ***Ought I to** report it to someone in authority?*
    ***Should** I report it to someone in authority?*
    ***Ought we to** make a start?*
    ***Should** we make a start?*

ought to
The contracted negative form is: *oughtn't (to)*. It is used informally.

    *Oh dear, we **oughtn't to** have let that happen.*
    *Well then she ought to do something about it, **oughtn't** she?*

Dare and need

The two verbs *dare* and *need* have characteristics of both modal verbs and main verbs. Because of this, they are called **semimodals**. They sometimes behave like modal verbs and do not add -s to the form that goes with **he**, **she**, and **it**. This means that they have no 3rd person singular inflection. They are then followed by the **base form** of a main verb.

> *Need I say more?*
> *Dare I ask how the project's going?*

The past form *needed* is not used as a modal; *dared* is occasionally used as a modal.

The modal uses of these verbs are all **negatives** or **questions**.

> *Where will you all be today? – Need you ask?*
> *You needn't come if you're busy.*
> *Dare I suggest that we start a sign-up sheet?*
> *I dare not tell him the truth; he'll go crazy.*

Questions using these verbs are often set expressions such as *Need I/ you ask?*, *Dare I suggest...?* and *Need I/we say more?*

Dare and *need* sometimes behave like main verbs with -s inflection. In this case they are followed by the *to* infinitive. They can also use the auxiliary *do* and have the whole range of tenses appropriate to a main verb.

> *Lisa doesn't need to know.*
> *Does Paul need to go now?*
> *Paul needs to go.*
> *Dare to be different!*
> *They don't dare to mention it to him.*

When *dare* or *need* are used as modal verbs in a positive **statement**, there must be a word of negative meaning in the same clause. This word can be outside the verb phrase and may be a word with a negative sense, such as *only, never, hardly.*

> He *need only* ask and I will tell him.
> *No* sensible driver *dare* risk that chance.

As a modal verb, *dare* has forms as follows:

I *dare* not *go*.	I *dared* not *go*.	I *didn't dare go*. (informal)
He *dare* not *go*.	He *dared* not *go*.	He *didn't dare go*. (informal)

Dare I *do* it?
Dare he *do* it?

As a main verb, *dare* has forms as follows:

I *dare to do* it.	I *do* not *dare to do* it.
He *dares to do* it.	He *did* not *dare to do* it.
He *does* not *dare to do* it.	*Does* he *dare to do* it?
He *doesn't dare to do* it.	*Doesn't* he *dare to do* it?

As a modal verb, *need* has forms as follows:

I *need* not *go*.	*Need* I *go*?
He *need* not *go*.	*Need* he *go*?
He *needn't* go.	*Needn't* he *go*?

As a main verb, *need* has forms as follows:

I *need* it.	I *need to do* it.
He *needs* it.	He *needs to do* it.
I *do* not *need to go*.	I *do* not *need to do* it.
He *does* not *need to go*.	*Does* he *need to go*?

- Either of the two forms of *dare* and *need* can be used for sentences that have the same meaning.

  > Anna **didn't dare to jump** off the high fence.
  > Anna **dared not jump** off the high fence.
  > You **don't need to come** if you don't want to.
  > You **needn't come** if you don't want to.

Used to

The verb *used to* is a "marginal" modal verb. Unlike the other modal verbs, it is only found in the past tense. Therefore, when it is used with *do* to make negatives and questions, the form of the auxiliary verb is always *did*.

Used to is used as follows:

– to describe an activity or a state that happened many times in the past. For positive sentences the meaning is similar to the use of *would* for habitual past actions, as described on page 54.

> *Gerry always **used to** go for a run before breakfast.*
> *Peter **didn't use to** say things like that when I knew him.*

– to refer to an activity or state that was true in the past but is no longer true.

> *I **used to** like rock climbing when I was younger.*
> *You **didn't use to** be so stressed!*

Used to takes the following forms:

– the form *used to* is used with all subjects e.g., *I, we, you, he, she, it, they*.

I **used to**	We **used to**
You **used to**	You **used to**
She **used to**	They **used to**

> *I **used to** live in New Jersey.*
> *He **used to** deliver newspapers but he owns the paper now.*
> *Nancy and Bill **used to** live in California.*

There are two forms for a negative:

– *did not/didn't use to*.

> We **didn't use to** have indoor plumbing when I was a child.
> Alan **did not use to** like children, but it's different now that he has his own.

– *used not to*.

> I **used not to** be able to watch myself on TV at all.
> We **used not to** worry much about money.

To form a question, use *did* + **subject** + *use to* + **base form**:
i.e., *did he use to...?*

> **Did they use to** visit you often? – Well, Mary **used to**.

The contracted negative form is *didn't use to*.

> Do not confuse *used to* + **base form** with *be used to* + **present participle**, where *used to* means *accustomed to*.
>
> > They lived in India for a long time, so they **are used to eating** spicy food.

Phrasal verbs

A **phrasal verb** is a type of verb that is created when a main verb is combined with either:

- an **adverb**,

  take off   *give in*
  blow up   *break down*

- a **preposition**,

  get at (someone)   *pick on* (someone)

- or an **adverb** + **preposition**,

  put up with (something)   *get out of* (doing something)

Type A. Verb plus adverb

Some Type A phrasal verbs have no object, i.e., they are **intransitive**. They make sense without any further addition to the verb.

> *Mary went away.*
> *Helen sat down.*
> *The students came back.*

Others require an object, i.e., they are **transitive**.

> *We could make out a figure in the distance.*
> *He tried to blow up the aircraft.*
> *Could you put your clothes away, please?*

If the object is a **noun**, many Type A phrasal verbs will allow the adverb to come either:

− before the object,

>   I *picked up* Jim *on my way home.*
>   He *blew out* the candle.
>   She *put away* her things.

− or after the object.

>   I *picked* Jim *up on my way home.*
>   He *blew* the candle *out*.
>   She *put* her things *away*.

If the object is a **pronoun**, it must come before the adverb.

>   I *picked* him *up*.
>   He *blew* it *out*.
>   She *put* them *away*.

Sometimes you can guess the meaning of these verbs from the meanings of the parts.

>   to *sit down* = sit + down
>   to *go away* = go + away

Sometimes you have to learn the new meanings, or use a dictionary.

>   to *make up* (an answer)   = invent
>   to *turn down* (an invitation) = decline
>   to *work out* (a problem)   = solve
>   to *put up* (a visitor)   = accommodate

Type B. Verb plus preposition

Type B phrasal verbs always have an object. This is because prepositions always have an object.

> *He asked for* the check.
> *He asked for* it.
> *She listened to* the doctor.
> *She listened to* her.
> *They referred to* our conversation.
> *They referred to* it.

Sometimes there are two objects: the object of the verb and the object of the preposition.

> *He asked* the waiter *for* the check.

Type C. Verb plus adverb and preposition

Type C phrasal verbs are a combination of the two previous kinds of verb. All the parts of a Type C phrasal verb come before the object.

> *We are looking forward to* our vacation/it.
> *Don't put up with* bad behavior/it.
> *You must look out for* the warning signs/them.

- It is sometimes hard to tell adverbs and prepositions apart, because often the same word can be both a preposition and an adverb, depending on how it is used. For further information about prepositions see p. 216.

The following are examples of the three types of phrasal verb that are explained on p. 80.

Type A

Phrasal verbs made from a verb plus an adverb may be intransitive (do not take an object) or transitive (take an object).

some phrasal verbs that do not take an object	*some phrasal verbs that do take an object*
to break down	to blow something up
to carry on	to break something off
to fall down	to bring a child up
to get about	to bring a subject up
to get up	to call something off
to give up	to clear something up
to go away	to close something down
to go off	to give something up
to go out	to leave something out
to grow up	to make something up
to hold on	to pick someone up

Type B

Phrasal verbs made from a verb plus a preposition are all transitive.

to add to something	to hope for something
to agree with someone	to insist on something
to apply for something	to laugh at something
to approve of something	to listen to something
to arrive at something	to live for something
to ask for something	to look for something
to believe in something	to look into something
to belong to someone	to pay for something
to call on someone	to refer to something
to care for someone	to rely on someone
to come across something	to run into someone
to deal with something	to run over something

Some Type B verbs are doubly transitive, since both the verb and the preposition can have an object.

> to **add** insult **to** injury
> to **ask** a first responder **for** help
> to **check** your answers **with** the teacher
> to **pay** the clerk **for** your groceries
> to **refer** a customer **to** the manager

Type C

Phrasal verbs with an adverb plus a preposition all take a prepositional object.

to put up with something	to keep away from something
to carry on with something	to look back on something
to catch up with something	to look forward to something
to check up on something	to look out for something
to come up with something	to look up to someone
to cut down on something	to make up for something
to do away with something	to put in for something
to face up to something	to run away with something
to fall back on something	to run out of something
to get along with someone	to run up against something
to get out of something	to stand up for something
to go back on something	to walk out on someone
to go in for something	to watch out for something
to break in on someone	to lead up to something

Tense

Time reference

Verb forms help us make reference to time through their **tense**. Tense shows whether an action or a state took place in the past or takes place in the present.

> Jessica **works** at the post office.
> Laurence **worked** at the post office over the Christmas holidays.

English has two **simple tenses** and six **compound tenses**.

Simple tenses

Verbs in simple tenses consist of a single word.

There is a **present simple** tense

> I like   I live
> you like   you live
> he likes   he lives

and a **past simple** tense.

> I liked   I lived
> you liked   you lived
> he liked   he lived

The simple tenses of regular verbs

The **present tense** is the same as the **base form** of the verb, except that an -s is added to the verb when it has a noun or he, she, or it as a subject. This is called the 3rd person singular form.

> he/she/it **likes**
> he/she/it **lives**

The **past tense** of a regular verb is made from the **base form** of the verb with -ed (or -d if the verb already ends in -e) added. The spelling is the same for all persons.

> I **liked**   I **lived**
> you **liked**   you **lived**
> he **liked**   he **lived**

The simple tenses of irregular verbs

Most irregular verbs make the **present tense** from the **base form** of the verb just as regular verbs do.

> Present
> I **find**   I **go**
> you **find**   you **go**
> he/she/it **finds** he/she/it **goes**

- Irregular verbs make the **past tense** in a number of different ways. Sometimes the past tense is a completely different word. See pp. 32–34 for more on irregular verbs.

> Past
> I **found**   I **went**
> you **found**   you **went**
> he/she/it **found** he/she/it **went**

Aspect

When we use a verb, we often need to refer to more than the time at which an event took place. We sometimes need to refer to actions and states as completed or not completed. **Aspect** describes the way we think of verbal actions.

The **continuous aspect** is formed by using the appropriate form of the auxiliary *be* together with the *-ing* form (**present participle**) of the main verb.

We use **continuous aspect** to show that an action:

– is going on at the time of speaking.

> I'm eating dinner just now. Can I call you back?
> I know what you are doing!
> Look! Someone's walking around in our driveway!

– was going on throughout the time that you are referring to.

> I was eating dinner when he called.
> I was waiting for her when she came out of the classroom.
> We were driving home when we saw the accident.

– will be going on at the time that you are referring to.

> We're going to Tennessee for vacation next year.
> They're coming to us for Christmas this year.

The **perfect aspect** is formed by using the appropriate form of the auxiliary *have* together with the *-ed* form (**past participle**) of the main verb.

We use **perfect aspect** to show that an action:

– is complete at the time of speaking.

> I **'ve finished** the book. It was great.
> We **'ve enjoyed** having you all to stay.
> Jo **has borrowed** the book, so I can't look at it now.

– was complete at the time you are referring to.

> I **had forgotten** my promise to Aunt Jane.
> Sharon **had lost** her key, so she had to wait outside.
> Sue **had seen** the film three times already.

– began in the past and continues in the present. This usage is for verbs that show states or conditions rather than single actions.

> I **'ve lived** with diabetes since childhood.
> She's never **appreciated** country and western music.
> Jill **has kept** all of Grandma's old photos.

> It is possible to have a compound tense that shows both aspects, continuous and perfect.
>
> Peter **has been talking** about you a lot recently.
> We **had been waiting** for 20 minutes and then three buses came.

Compound tenses

The compound tenses are a combination of present or past **tense** (shown through an auxiliary verb) with continuous or perfect **aspect**. See also pp. 87–88.

> I'm **doing** my homework at the moment, so I can't come out.
> Ben **has seen** the camera that he wants.
> She **was listening** to the radio.
> Sandra **had invited** all her friends.

- The tense of the auxiliary verb shows whether the compound verb is **present** tense,

> I'm **eating** dinner just now; I'll call you back.
> We've **had** a fantastic stay; thank you.

or **past** tense.

> We **were dancing** around the living room and singing along.
> Mom **had gone** out and left us some snacks.

The choice of the **auxiliary** and the **participle** expresses the aspect of the verb.

- the auxiliary *be* and the *-ing* participle (the present participle) show the **continuous** aspect .

> My brother **is having** a party tomorrow.
> The kids **were running** wild when we got home.

- the auxiliary *have* and the *-ed* participle (the past participle) show the **perfect** aspect.

> Juanita **has walked** more than 500 miles for charity.
> Someone **had tied up** the dog to keep it from wandering off.

These are the main compound tenses:

present continuous   = present of *be* + *-ing* participle.

   Kerry is waiting until Jessica gets here.

past continuous   = past of *be* + *-ing* participle.

   Maria was watching TV when Jo called.

present perfect   = present of *have* + *-ed* participle.

   Sam has seen a few things that he'd like to buy.
   We've bought some better equipment.

past perfect   = past of have + *-ed* participle.

   She had really believed their story!
   Rory had had enough of their silly questions.

A compound verb can also combine both the continuous and perfect aspects, using **two auxiliary verbs** and a **main verb**. This produces the following combinations:

present perfect continuous
   = present of *have* + past participle of *be* + *-ing* participle.

   For the past two months, Zoe has been visiting us once a week.
   We've been trying to finish that job since Easter.

past perfect continuous
   = past of *have* + past participle of *be* + *-ing* participle.

   Vicky had been hoping for better news.
   I had been traveling all day, so I was exhausted.

The modal auxiliaries can be used in compound tenses.

> She **might be babysitting** for us on Friday.
> We **would be sitting** here for hours if I told you everything.
> I **may have eaten** something that disagreed with me.
> I expect Nayeema **will have bought** something for supper.

Modal auxiliaries come in first position in the verb phrase, so they are followed by:

– the subject and the rest of the verb in questions.

> **Will you be going** shopping after work?

– the negative *not* and the rest of the verb in negative statements.

> Marcus **may not have been** entirely truthful.

– the subject, the negative *not*, and the rest of the verb in negative questions.

> **Will you not be pushing** for that to be changed?

However, if the contracted negative form of the modal is used, then it comes before the subject and the rest of the verb.

> **Won't he be visiting** us this evening?

> Modals are not used with the supporting auxiliary verb *do*.

See pp. 58–79 for the meanings and uses of modal auxiliary verbs.

Responses

When you respond to a question that contains a compound verb phrase, you usually use just the first part of the verb phrase. That is, you use one of the auxiliary verbs.

If it is a simple tense you use the supporting auxiliary *do*.

> *Do you like avocados? – Yes, I do*.

If one of the forms of *be* or *have* is the first verb in the verb phrase, then use that as the response form.

> *Has Claire been here yet? – Yes, she has*.
> *Was Sue Ellen asking for help? – Yes, she was*.

If a **modal** verb is first in the verb phrase, some speakers prefer to use the modal and the auxiliary form together as the response form.

> *Do you think he might have left the parcel somewhere? –*
>   *Yes, he might or Yes, he might have*.
> *So Laurence could be coming with us then. – Yes, he could*
>   *or Yes, he could be*.

The present simple tense

This tense has only two typical forms: the base form, and the third-person singular form with added **-s**:

> *I know her.*
> *He knows her.*

The present simple tense of *do* is used as the supporting auxiliary when you want to:

− ask a question,

> ***Do*** *I know you?*
> ***Does*** *she know you?*

− make a negative statement using *not*,

> *I* ***do not*** *know her.*
> *She* ***does not*** *know you.*

− or give a short response.

> ***Do*** *you just* ***have*** *coffee for breakfast? – Yes, I* ***do***.

We use the present simple tense to talk about:

− habits, likes and dislikes, and things that happen regularly.

> *I* ***like*** *coffee for breakfast but everyone else in my family* ***prefers*** *tea.*
> *I* ***don't take*** *sugar in my coffee.*
> *What* ***does*** *Jamie* ***usually have*** *for breakfast?*
> *They* ***often go*** *to the movies* ***on Saturdays***.
> *I* ***don't usually watch*** *TV.*

(When we talk about habits, we often add adverbs such as *often*, *always*, *usually*, *sometimes*, or *never*, or adverbial phrases such as *on Sundays* or *in the summer*.)

– statements of fact that are scientific truths or that are about a permanent state.

> *The sun **rises** in the east.*
> *Birds **fly** south in the winter.*
> *We **live** in Iowa.*

– statements that indicate the speaker's opinions or beliefs.

> *I **think** he's a very good teacher.*
> *I **don't agree** with that at all.*

– for dramatic narrative to tell a story or describe an action vividly.

> *He **walks** slowly to the checkout and **puts** his bag on the counter.*
> *As the cashier **opens** the drawer he **pulls out** a gun...*

– or when giving a commentary on a sports event or public function.

> *... but Nadal **sees** it. He **runs** up to the net and **smashes** the ball.*

We can also use the present simple for planned future actions with a time adverb; for example, to talk about travel plans and schedules. See pp. 110–117 for more about future reference.

> *The train for Hartford **leaves** at 10:40 a.m. and **arrives** at 3:30 p.m.*

We use the present simple in conditional sentences about real possibilities that affect the future. See p. 272 for more on conditional sentences.

> *If I **lend** you my notes, I won't be able to review tonight.*

The present simple is typically used for verbs related to the things you do with your senses (i.e., hearing, smell, vision, etc.).

> I **smell** garlic.
> Do you **hear** that noise?
> I **see** several houses on the horizon.

The past simple tense

The past tense form is the same for all persons, and for singular and plural:

> I **met** her.
> They **met** him.
> I **went** there.
> They **went** there.

Because the past simple consists of one word only, the past simple tense of **do**, which is **did**, is used as the supporting auxiliary when you want to:

— ask a question,

> **Did** I **meet** him?
> **Did** they **meet** him?
> **Did** I **go** there?
> **Did** it **go** there?

— make a negative statement using **not**,

> I **did** not **meet** her.
> They **did** not **meet** her.
> I **did** not **go** there.
> They **did** not **go** there.

— or make a response.

> Did you see Jenny yesterday? – No, I **didn't**.
> Did Peggy phone you ? – Yes, she **did**.

We use the past simple tense to talk about:

– single actions in the past.

> He **locked** the door and **left** the house.
> I **went** out and **brought** the cat back in again.

– habitual actions in the past, often with *always*, *never*, or *often*.

> In those days I **always went** to Juliano's for lunch.
> I **cycled** in **every day** and that soon **made** me fit.
> I **often visited** New York on business when I was in publishing.

– past actions where a definite time is mentioned. It is often used with a time expression such as *ago* or *last month*, when the action is seen as finished.

> **Some time ago** now, I **went** to Aruba for a month.
> **Once upon a time** there was a king in a faraway land.
> I **saw** Roger **a little while back**.
> I **bought** the microwave **a year ago**.

– points where the main action is broken. The rest of the sentence uses the past continuous tense to describe the past activity or action.

> I was clearing out the garage when a car **came** up the drive.
> We were leaving the house when the phone **rang**.

The present continuous tense

The verb *be* varies according to person in forms of the present continuous tense:

> *I am winning.*
> *He is winning.*
>
> *Am I winning?*
> *Is she winning?*
>
> *I am not winning.*
> *He is not winning.*
>
> *Aren't I winning?*
> *Isn't she winning?*
>
> *Am I not winning?*
> *Is she not winning?*

Some main verbs are not normally used in the continuous in standard American or British English, though they may be used this way in other varieties of English. These are generally verbs about states rather than actions, or verbs that pertain to perception and the five senses.

> *I am winning.*   **but not** *I am liking it.*
> *There is a bird singing.*   **but not** *I am hearing it.*

We use the present continuous tense to talk about:

– things that are happening now, at the time when we are talking.

> *Mom's **mowing** the lawn, but Ibrahim **isn't doing** anything.*
> *The children aren't asleep; they**'re messing around**.*
> *Come on; you**'re not trying**.*

– a temporary activity, even if it is not happening at the time when you are talking.

I'm studying German in college.
I'm thinking of getting a new car.

– a temporary situation in contrast to a permanent situation.

I'm living in Pittsburgh at the moment.
Francesca is working in the stables over the holidays.

– a changing state or situation.

My headache is getting better.
The daylight is slowly fading.

– the circumstances under which something is generally done.

I have to wear glasses when I'm driving.

– arrangements for future events along with a time adverb or phrase.

I am flying to New York next week.

See p. 110 for more on the future.

We also use it to express annoyance at a repeated action. In this case, one of the following adverbs is used with the verb: always, forever, constantly, continually.

She's always whining about something.
He's forever laughing and making dumb jokes.

When you give a short answer to a question, it is normal to echo (that is, repeat) the auxiliary but not the main verb.

Are you waiting for someone? – Yes, I am.
Is Hamid working in the library? – No, he isn't.

The past continuous tense

The verb *be* varies according to person in forms of the past continuous tense:

> *I was winning.*
> *She was winning.*
> *They were winning.*

> *Was I winning?*
> *Was she winning?*
> *Were you winning?*

> *I was not winning*
> *We were not winning.*
> *They weren't winning.*

Some main verbs are not typically used in the continuous in standard American and British English, though they may be used this way in other varieties of English. These are generally verbs about states rather than feelings and about perception and the five senses.

We use the past continuous tense in these ways:

– with a time expression, such as *at 6 p.m. yesterday*, to talk about an action that began before that time and finished after it. The exact length of time the action took is not important.

> *What **were you doing** at eight o'clock last night? –*
> *I **was standing** at the bus stop.*

– to talk about an interrupted action. Note that for the event that interrupts the action, we use the past simple tense.

> *We **were** all **sitting** in our places when the bell **rang**.*

– to talk about a short action that happened while a longer one was already taking place.

   *I **dropped** my purse while I **was waiting** for the bus.*

– to describe a scene in the past, especially in a story.

   *It was a dreadful morning. The snow **was still falling**, the wind **was blowing**, and the cars **were skidding** off the icy roads.*

The present perfect tense

The verb *have* varies according to person for the present perfect tense; it is often contracted:

> I *have finished*.
> He *has found* them.
> They*'ve finished*.
> They*'ve found* her.
> Listen! I*'ve heard* some great news; Jim*'s won*!
> They*'ve bought* a brand new car.
> You*'ve got* a lot of nerve!

> *Have* they *finished*? – No, they *haven't*.
> *Has* Mary *arrived* yet? – No, she *hasn't*.

> I *have* not *finished*.
> He *has* not *finished*.
> Ranee *hasn't found* her bracelet yet.
> They *haven't seen* her.

The contracted forms are:

has = **'s**	have = **'ve**
has not = **hasn't**	have not = **haven't**

The present perfect tense is used to talk about events that are relevant to the present but that happened in the past. It is also used to talk about an action that started in the past, without mentioning a specific time.

> Her daughter *has had* an accident.
> We *have seen* the Eiffel Tower and the Arc de Triomphe.

If the present perfect occurs more than once in a compound sentence, the second and subsequent instances of *have* can be left out.

> They *have bought* their tickets and *chosen* their seats.

- We can use *just* if we want to show that the action has very recently been completed.

  > They **have just bought** their tickets.
  > He **has just finished** his homework.

If an event did not take place but is possible in theory you can use *never* with the present perfect. If you want to find out whether something took place or not, you can use *ever*.

  > **Have** you **ever been** to Greece?
  > I**'ve never done** anything like this before.

- If we want to indicate a moment in time or a period of time, we can use expressions such as *recently*, *lately*, *this morning*, *today*, or *this week* with the present perfect tense.

  > I **haven't been** to the movies **recently**.
  > I**'ve waited a week** for your answer.

- In questions and negative sentences, the present perfect can be used with *yet*, meaning "at the time of speaking." In positive sentences, use *already*.

  > **Haven't** you **finished yet**?
  > **Have** you **bought** the tickets **yet**?
  > I**'ve** already **seen** that movie.

The present perfect tense is often used to answer the question *How long...?* together with *for* to talk about a period of time, or *since* to talk about duration from a point in time.

  > I **have lived** in Savannah **for fifteen years**.
  > **How long have you lived** in Savannah?
  > We**'ve had** this car **since** 2008.
  > We **haven't spoken** to each other **since** the night of the argument.

The past perfect tense

The past tense form had, along with the past participle, is used to form the past perfect tense:

> *I had misunderstood.*
> *She had misunderstood.*
> *I had finished.*
> *She had found them.*
> *She'd gone.*
> *They'd found her.*

> *Had I misunderstood?*
> *Had it gone?*
> *Had Mary arrived before Peter told you? – No, she hadn't.*

> *I had not misunderstood.*
> *He had misunderstood.*
> *I had not finished.*
> *It had not worked.*
> *I hadn't realized how serious the problem was.*
> *They hadn't seen her.*

The contracted forms are:

> had = **'d**   had not = **hadn't**

The past perfect tense goes one step further back into the past than the present perfect.

> *Had you ever seen her before then? – No, I hadn't.*

The past perfect tense is used to talk about:

– an action that took place in the past before something else took place.

> She **had just made** some coffee when I arrived.

– an action or state that began before another action in the past and continued up to the time of the second action and perhaps even beyond that time.

> Ashraf **had** already **known** my brother **for two years** when I met him.

● It is often used in the main clause of a complex sentence, to set the scene for a past event.

> We **had wanted** to visit Canada **for a long time**, so last year we decided to go.

● It is often used with a time expression such as *always* or for *several days*.

> We **had been** away **for several days** when the burglary occurred.

The present perfect continuous tense

The present perfect continuous is formed with *have been* or *has been*
followed by a present participle:

> *I have been waiting.*
> *I've been waiting.*
> *She has been waiting.*
> *She's been waiting.*

> *Have I been snoring?*
> *Has he been waiting?*
> *Have you been waiting long?*

> *I have not been waiting.*
> *She has not been waiting.*

We use the present perfect continuous tense to talk about:

– actions and states that began in the past and are still continuing
  at the time of speaking or writing.

> *I have been holding this ladder for ages. When are you going to
>   come down?*

– actions and states that began in the past and have just finished.

> *Thank goodness you're here! I've been waiting for hours.*

– repeated actions.

> *I've been getting this magazine for years now.*
> *We've been attending church weekly since last fall.*

There is sometimes little difference between the meaning of the present perfect and the meaning of the present perfect continuous when they are used for long-term actions.

> *I have been working here for three years.*
> *I have worked here for three years.*

We usually choose the continuous form for more temporary actions or states.

> *I have been living in Phoenix since I finished college.*

... and the present perfect form for more permanent ones.

> *I have lived in Phoenix since I was born.*

- We cannot use this tense with verbs such as *be*, *know*, and *like*, which are not used in continuous forms. It is also not typically used for verbs that pertain to the five senses.

- We can use *for* and *since* with the continuous form in the same way as with the present perfect form.

> *I have been studying English for three years.*
> *I have studied English for three years.*

> *I have been living in Phoenix since I finished college.*
> *I have lived in Phoenix since I was born.*

See also pp. 98–101 for more about continuous uses of the verb.

The past perfect continuous tense

The past perfect continuous is formed with *had been* followed by a
present participle:

> *I had been waiting.*
> *I'd been waiting.*
> *She had been waiting.*
> *She'd been waiting.*

> *Had I been talking nonsense? What had I said?*
> *Had he been waiting long?*
> *Had you been expecting to meet Mary at the airport?*

> *I had not been waiting.*
> *She had not been waiting.*
> *They hadn't been looking very carefully.*

The past perfect continuous tense is used to talk about an action which
began before another action in the past and either:

– continued up to the time of the second action,

> *I hadn't been waiting long when a bus came up beside me.*

– or was completed before the second action happened.

> *I had been studying and decided to take a stroll to clear my mind.*
> *We had been cleaning the house for hours, so we stopped and had
>   a drink.*

● The past perfect continuous is often used in the main clause of
  a complex sentence, to set the scene for an event.

> *I had been driving for about an hour when I heard a noise in
>   the engine.*

- The past perfect continuous is often used to talk about a repeated action.

    *She **had been trying** to phone her mother all day.*

> Remember that you cannot use the past perfect continuous with verbs such as *like*, which are not used in the continuous. See p. 98.

Future reference

Verb forms

English has no future tense as such. However, several forms, especially
the **modal** verb *will*, can be used to make future reference. These forms
are summarized as follows:

1 *Will* + the **base form** makes the most direct form of future reference.
See p. 66. The other modal verbs that express possibility make a more
indirect reference to future time.

> *It **will take** several years to finish.*
> *Jean **will take care of** the dogs while we're away.*
> *I'll **tell** her to mind her own business.*
> *We'll **see**.*

2 *Be going to* + the **base form** is used to express intention and make
predictions. See p. 112.

> *He failed his exams last year; this year he **is going to work** harder.*
> *You'd better get the dogs in; it **is going to rain**.*

3 The **present continuous tense** is used to talk about plans and
arrangements in the future with a time adverb. See p. 98.

> *Sarah and Harriet **are meeting** at ten o'clock on Tuesday.*
> *I **am flying** to Mobile on Friday.*

4 The **present simple tense** is used with a time adverb to talk about
future plans that are part of a schedule or previous arrangement.
See p. 93.

> *The main feature **starts** at 2:45 p.m.*
> *We **leave** at 4 p.m. tomorrow.*

5   The **future perfect tense** (*will have* + the **past participle**) is used
with a time adverb to talk about an action that will be finished at the
time in the future that you are referring to. See p. 115.

> *I was hoping to meet James, but by the time I arrive he* **will have**
> **gone** *home.*

6   *Be about to* + the **base form** is used to talk about the very near future.
See p. 116.

> *I'm sorry I can't stop and chat; I'**m about to leave** for work.*

7   The **future continuous tense** (*will be* + the **present participle**) is
used to talk about future action in progress. See p. 117.

> *What* **will** *you* **be doing** *on Saturday morning? Oh, I'll* **be**
> **shopping** *as usual.*

8   *Be to* + the **base form** is used to talk about formal plans, especially
in journalism. See p. 117.

> *The President* **is to attend** *the UN general assembly tomorrow.*

1   ***will***

The modal verb *will* followed by the **base form** of a main verb is used
to refer to the future.

> *I* **will come**.   *We* **will come**.
> *You* **will come**.   *You* **will come**.
> *She/he/it* **will come**.   *They* **will come**.

Some older or more traditional speakers may prefer to use *shall* in the
1st person singular and plural. See p. 66 for more details.

- The contracted form is '*ll* for both **will** and **shall**, so there is no difference in informal speech.

    I'll probably be late, but I expect they'll be on time.

The contracted negative forms are **won't** and **shan't**. *Shan't* is not used in contemporary American English.

*We **won't come**.*

- If there are two verbs in the sentence, it is normal not to repeat the modal form before the second one.

    *I **won't go** see him or **speak** to him for six months.*

We use **will** (or rarely, **shall**) for future reference in the following ways:

- to talk about future facts.

    *I **won't see** Mary next week.*
    *I'll **be** on the plane this time tomorrow.*

- to make promises or reassurances.

    *I'll **be** home in time for supper.*
    *This **won't happen** again, I can assure you.*

- to announce a decision that the speaker has just made.

    *I'll **have** the pizza and a side salad, please.*
    *OK, I'll **ask** him, and see if his story matches yours.*

- to express negative intention, using **won't**.

    *I **won't go** there again. The service was dreadful.*

– to express refusal.

> I **won't put up with** any more of this silly behavior.
> I've tried to persuade her but she **won't come**.

– to talk about an event in the future, possibly in the distant future. A time clause may be used.

> People **will be** amazed when they hear about this in years to come.

– to refer to inevitable actions or events that will take place in the future.

> Christmas is past, but it **will come** again next year.

– to express an opinion about a future event after verbs such as believe, expect, hope, know, and think.

> I **expect** he'**ll be** home soon.
> I **hope** you'**ll be** very happy in your new home.

– to express a real possibility in conditional sentences. See p. 272.

> If you call after six I'**ll tell** you all about it.

2 *be going to*
Future reference can be made with *be* + *going to* + the **base form** of a main verb.

> I *am going to wait*.
> He *is going to wait*.
> I *am not going to wait*.
> He *is not going to wait*.
> Is he *going to wait*?
> Are they *going to wait*?

Be going to is used in the following ways:

– to express intention about the future.

> Mary **isn't going** to study art; she**'s going** to be a nurse.

– to talk about things that have already been decided.

> Is Jim **going to leave** his job? – Yes, **he is**.
> Where's Mary? She said she **was going to come** early.

– to make a prediction about the future, often the very near future, based on something in the present.

> Watch the milk! It **is going to boil** over!
> Sally never does any work; she **is going to fail** her exams.

If the past tense of *be* is used, a past intention or prediction can be expressed.

> Judy **was going to meet** me, but she was ill and couldn't come.
> She **was** obviously **going to get** blisters with those new shoes.

Note this difference:

Be going to is usually used for future events where the speaker expresses his or her intention, often about something already decided.
Will is used to express decisions made at the moment of speaking.

> I'm **going to go** to the movies on Friday; would you like to come?
> Yes, I'**ll go** if Chris goes.
> No thanks, I'm **going to visit** my uncle this weekend.

3 Present continuous

The present continuous tense is used to talk about plans for the future, or specific arrangements that people have made for future events.

> *The school **is having** a bake sale next week; I'**m organizing** it.*

It is often used in questions about future arrangements.

> *What **are you doing** on Saturday? – I'**m going** to a football game with Peter.*
> *When **are you leaving** college? – At the end of semester.*

If there are two verbs in the sentence, it is normal not to repeat the auxiliary before the second and subsequent ones.

> *We **are meeting** at 12:30 p.m., **having** a quick lunch, and **starting** work at 1:15.*

4 Present simple

The present simple tense is also used to talk about events that form part of a schedule or program.

> *The flight **leaves** Albuquerque at 10:10 a.m. and **arrives** in Baltimore at 5:20 p.m.*
> *These are the arrangements for Friday: doors **open** at 7 p.m., the Mayor **arrives** at 7:30 p.m., and the meeting **starts** at 7:45 p.m.*

5 The future perfect (*will have* + the past participle of a main verb)

This form is used to talk about an action that will be complete at a time in the future that you are talking about. It is often used with verbs relating to finishing or completing. The contracted positive form is *'ll have* or **will've**.

> *Can you come over next Saturday? – Yes,* **I'll have finished** *my exams by then.*
> *Dad* **will've made** *dinner by the time we get back.*

The contracted negative is won't have.

> *The essay is due on Tuesday, but I* **won't have completed** *it by then.*

In questions, the subject comes after will. The short answer to a question that begins with will is will without the past participle.

> *Will you* **have finished** *dinner by then? – Yes,* **we will**.

6 *be* + *about to* + the base form

The appropriate form of *be* + *about to* + the **base form** of a main verb is used to talk about events in the very near future.

> *Turn off the burner! The soup* **is about to boil** *over.*
> *Come on! The film's* **about to start**!

It is sometimes used with *just* following the *be* form to give even more immediacy.

> *I* **was (just) about to leave** *when the phone rang.*

Be about to can also be used in the **past** to suggest that someone is *on the point of* carrying out an action when it is interrupted. In this case it is usually followed by *when*.

*They **were** (just) **about to go** to bed **when** the fire started.*

7 The future continuous tense

This is made with ***will*** + ***be*** + the **present participle** of a main verb. *Will be* forms negatives, contractions, questions, and short answers in the usual way, as shown on page 67.

The future continuous is used in an informal way to suggest that something is about to happen or will happen at some time that is not clear or precise.

> *I'll **be seeing** you.*
> *We'll **be getting** in touch with you.*
> *They'll **be wanting** us to clean our own classrooms next!*
> *We **won't be seeing** Uncle John while we are in Tucson.*

It is also used to talk about an activity that will already be in progress at a particular time in the future.

> ***Will** you **be working** here next week?*
> *No, I won't. I'll **be starting** my new job.*
> *Just think! This time next week, we **will be flying** to Cancun.*

8 *be to* + the base form

The appropriate form of *be* + *to* + the **base form** of a main verb is used mainly in fairly formal English to talk about plans, arrangements, and instructions. It indicates that what will happen is part of an expected process, and is often found in journalistic texts.

> *Foreign ministers of the NATO countries **are to meet** in Brussels next week.*
> *The funeral **is to take place** on Saturday.*

Active and passive

Active sentences

In the following example, the verb is **active**.

> *The post office delivers thousands of letters every day.*

In a sentence with an active verb, the subject of the sentence carries out the action. This is sometimes called the active voice. We use the active voice when the subject of the verb is the doer of the action. The active is used in most English speech and writing, because we usually want to inform our listener or our reader who or what did something.

> *He hid the money under the bed.*
> *The car knocked over a pedestrian.*
> *I'm sending the book by courier.*

Passive sentences

In the following example, the verb is **passive**.

> *Thousands of letters are delivered every day.*

The subject in a passive sentence is not the person or thing that does the action of the verb. It is the person or thing that the verb acts on or does something to. Sentences with a passive verb use the passive voice.

> *The injured man was helped by first responders.*
> *The man was being questioned by the police.*
> *The patient was operated on by a team of five surgeons.*

The passive is made with the appropriate form of *be* + the **past participle** of the main verb.

- We use the passive voice to direct our listener's attention to a different part of our message. For instance, in the first example of this section we do not need to know who delivers the letters, so all mention of the letter carrier or the post office is left out.

- The passive can be used when we do not know who performs an action, or when it is not important to know. It is sometimes much more important to know what has happened than who or what did it.

> *The money **was hidden** under the bed.*
> *The book **is being sent** by courier.*
> *An elderly man **was run over** while crossing the road.*
> *Roger **has been given** his promotion.*
> *The patient **was operated on**.*

The passive allows us to select the parts of a sentence that we wish to draw attention to. It can be used when we want to focus on:

- the **agent**, i.e., who performed the action or brought it about. We show the agent with *by*.

> *The window was broken **by some boys**.*
> *My brother was given extra lessons **by his teacher**.*
> *The old man was run over **by a careless driver**.*
> *The patient was operated on **by a team of top surgeons**.*

- the **instrument**, i.e., what was used to make the action happen. We show the instrument using *by* or *with*.

> *The sorting is done **by machine**.*
> *The safe was blown open **with dynamite**.*
> *The old man was knocked over **by a bus**.*
> *I was showered **with presents** on my eighteenth birthday.*

– the **means**, i.e., what caused the action to happen. We show the means using *by* or *with*. There is sometimes very little difference between means and instrument.

> *The window was shattered **by the explosion**.*
> *He was exhausted **with the strain of caring for his elderly parents**.*
> *Spelling errors are marked **with an X in the margin**.*
> *He was taken to a hospital **by ambulance**.*

The subject of a passive verb

The subject of a passive verb is the word that would be its object in a sentence with an active verb. When a verb has two objects, either the indirect object or the direct object of the active verb may become the subject of the passive verb.

> ***I've been offered** a job in Kuwait.*
> ***We were given** a second chance.*

If the indirect object is mentioned after the passive verb, the sentence must use *to*.

> *The building **has been sold to** property developers.*
> *The medal **is awarded to** students who have shown academic excellence.*

Some verbs that are often used this way are: *give, offer, lend, promise, sell,* and *tell*.

Form of the passive
Passive verbs are made from a form of *be* + the **past participle** of a main verb. In the passive, the form of the auxiliary verb *be* indicates the tense.

>They **sell** cheap computer games here.
>Cheap computer games **are sold** here.
>They **took** him to the police station for questioning.
>He **was taken** to the police station for questioning.

- Some verbs are only or mostly used in the passive, e.g., *be born* and *be deemed*.

>The movie **was deemed** unsuitable for younger audiences.
>My brother and I **were born** in Utah.

The impersonal passive

This form of the passive sentence is useful when you want to report what is or was generally understood or accepted by a group of people.

>The suitcase **was found** to be empty.
>The money **is thought** to be missing.
>The rumor **is believed** to be true.

The form *it* + **passive** + **that** can be used when you do not want to mention the source of information.

>**It is reported** that over a hundred people died in the explosion.
>**It is said** that his income is over $200 a minute.

The passive with *get*

In informal English, a type of passive is sometimes made with *get* instead of *be*.

>How did that teapot **get broken**?
>Our cat **got run over** last week.

Get is also used to form a small set of passive verbs in contexts which are not informal (or "neutral"), e.g., *get dressed*, *get married*, *get lost*.

> *Harriet got lost in the subway.*
> *When are you two getting married?*

For both of these uses of get the usual past participle is gotten in American English.

> *He'd just gotten his hair cut when I saw him.*

The causative passive with *have*

There is another verbal group that is like the passive, because the person who carries out the action of the main verb is not the person who is the subject of the clause. It expresses the idea that the subject caused or ordered someone else to do something.

> Compare:
>
> *Ralph repaired his car* = Ralph did the work.
> *Ralph had his car repaired* = He paid someone else to do the work.
>
> > *We are having the garage door replaced.*
> > *She had her hair cut short.*
> > *They did not have the carpet cleaned after all.*

This construction has the form: *have* + **direct object** + **past participle**. A more informal version of this verbal group uses *get* + **direct object** + **past participle**.

> *We are getting the garage door replaced.*
> *She got her hair cut short.*
> *They didn't get the carpet cleaned after all.*

Finite and nonfinite verbs

In a sentence, there is normally at least one verb that has both a **subject** and a **tense**. When a verb has a subject and a tense, it can be referred to as a **finite** verb.

> *We want* Charlie to act as club secretary.
> *I like* taking photographs of insects.
> *Coming home last night, I saw* a deer run across the road.

Some forms of a verb are referred to as **nonfinite**. The **present** and **past participles** and the **to infinitive** are the most common of these. The base form is often used in a nonfinite way. Every verb can be used in a clause in either a **finite** or **nonfinite** way.

- A verb is finite if it is used in a clause in combination with a subject and a tense.

  > *I walked* home.
  > *We saw* a deer.
  > *They appreciate* a little praise now and then.

- It is nonfinite if it is used:

- without the verb having a tense.

  > *To open*, tear off the tab.
  > *Looking* around, he noticed a letter on the floor.
  > *Worn out* by the heat, they stopped for a drink.

- with no agreement between the subject (if there is one) and the verb.

  > *That plan failing*, he gave up.
  > *Our guest having departed*, we felt a little depressed.

A compound verb is actually made up of one finite part, which is always the first auxiliary verb, while the remaining nonfinite parts are the base form or the participles.

In the following examples the finite part of the verb phrase is in blue italic:

> I *may* **have been joking** *when I* **said** *that.*
> Helen *was* **running** *around screaming.*
> I *had* **been living** *in a dream for months.*
> Olivia *is* **coming** *over at 6 o'clock this evening.*

The present simple and past simple forms of a verb are always finite.

> I *sing*.
> We **tell** *stories at night.*
> Maya **laughed**.
> The shelter **collapsed**.

• A nonfinite verb is sometimes used immediately after a finite verb.

> I *like* **to get up** *early on weekends.*
> Harriet really **dislikes** **cleaning** *the oven.*
> I certainly **wouldn't want** **to see** *him again.*
> We **persuaded** *them* **to join** *us.*

Often a noun or pronoun can come between the finite verb and the nonfinite one. See p. 128 and p. 129 for more on this.

> We **want** *Charlie* **to act** *as club secretary.*
> She **saw** *houses* **destroyed** *by the tornado.*
> I don't **like** *you* **cleaning** *your boots over the sink.*

- When the second verb is an *-ing* form coming after a noun or pronoun, there can be a difference in grammar between two similar sentences. Both sentences below are acceptable, although the first example might seem ambiguous to some people. In the second sentence, the *-ing* form is used as a verbal noun, not a participle. See also p. 130.

    *She didn't like **him** cleaning his boots over the sink.*
    *She didn't like **his** cleaning his boots over the sink*

The nonfinite parts of the verb

Nonfinite parts of a verb are those that do not indicate number, person or tense. The common nonfinite forms are:

- the **base form** (sometimes called the **bare infinitive**)
- the **present participle** or -*ing* form
- the **past participle**
- the *to* **infinitive**

There are also other nonfinite forms, such as:

- the **continuous** *to* **infinitive**: *to be teaching*
- the **perfect** *to* **infinitive**: *to have taught*
- the **passive** *to* **infinitive**: *to be taught*

The base form

As well as serving as the verb form on which most of the other parts of the verb are based, the **base form** is frequently used as a nonfinite part of the verb. Because of this it is sometimes called the "*bare infinitive*" or the "*infinitive without to.*"

The **base form** is used as a **nonfinite** part of the verb in these ways:

- after modal verbs.

    *You must **stop** at the curb before you cross.*
    *He should **think** before he speaks.*

- after *let's* (suggestion) and *let* (permission) and *make* (compulsion).

    ***Let's invite** Annette over for dinner.*
    ***Let** the cat **go**!*
    ***Make** him **stop**!*
    ***Let** him **finish** what he was saying!*

− after *feel, hear, see, watch* + an object.

> I **heard** him **run** downstairs.
> Later we **saw** them **leave** the house.

− after a **to** infinitive to which it is joined by *and*.

> I want you to sit and **listen**.
> Just wait and **see**.

− after imperatives *come* and *go*; these uses are informal.

> Go **see** who is at the door.
> Come **sit** beside me for a while.

− after *would rather* and *had better*.

> I would rather **go** out, but I think we had better **stay** home and finish the painting.

Verbs of perception may be followed either by the **base form** or by the **-ing** form. There is often a difference of meaning between the two.

These verbs include: *see, hear, feel, smell, listen to, watch*.

> We watched her **park** the car = we watched the whole event.
> We watched her **parking** the car = we may only have seen part of the event.
> I heard a owl **call** = I heard just one call.
> We heard the birds **singing** = We heard part of the song of the birds.

The *to* infinitive

The *to* infinitive is used as follows:

– after an adjective of quality such as *small*, *tall*, *agreeable*, *pleasant*, *funny* that is used in combination with *too*.

> The child was **too small to reach** the switch.
> The knife was **too dull to cut** the string.

or (*not*) + adjective of quality + *enough*.

> The child was **not tall enough to reach** the switch.
> The knife was **not sharp enough to cut** the string.
> I was **stupid enough to go** walking in flip-flops.

– after adjectives of emotion such as: *angry*, *happy*, *glad*, *sad*, *sorry*, *surprised*, to express the reason for the emotion.

> I'm **glad to see** you.
> I'm **sorry to hear** your news.

– after a "behavior" adjective such as: *good*, *kind*, *nice*, *stupid*, *wrong*, (sometimes + *of* + another **noun phrase**).

> It was **good of you to come**, and **kind of Jane to have sent** those flowers.
> It was **stupid to shout** like that.
> It was **kind of you to call** me.

– after a **WH-** word such as: *how*, *what*, *where*, *whether*, *which*, *who*, *whom*.

> We have no idea **what to get** for Tim's birthday.
> I don't know **where to go**.
> I can't think **how to do it**.
> They were wondering **who to see** first.

- after a noun phrase such as *a good idea*, *a good thing*, *a mistake* (sometimes + **for** + another **noun phrase**).

  It was a mistake for Jim to buy that motorbike.
  It was a good idea to stop here.

- after an adjective such as *easy, difficult, hard, impossible* + *for* + **noun phrase**.

  It has never been easy for David to take exams.

- after a verb followed by for, e.g., *ask, wait* + *for* + **noun phrase**.

  They are waiting for us to decide.

- The *to* infinitive can be used to express purpose or necessity after a verb followed by a pronoun or a noun.

  purpose: I brought *it to read* on the flight = so that I could read it.
  necessity: There is *work to do*! = work that must be done.

Sometimes the particle *to* can be used alone; for example, in a short response when the whole verb form was used earlier.

  Did you meet Tina? No, I wanted to, but she was wasn't there.
  Are you going to visit the museum? Yes, we hope to.

The *to* infinitive and the *-ing* form

The *to* infinitive and the *-ing* form (the present participle) can each be used after certain verbs.

Verbs followed by the *to* infinitive include: *agree, arrange, attempt, choose, decide, fail, hope, learn, manage, offer, plan, seem.*

> I **agreed to help** Shona with her homework.
> The driver **attempted to remove** the flat tire.
> I **hope to see** you again at the next meeting.

Verbs followed by an **object** + the *to* **infinitive** include: *advise, allow, command, forbid, force, invite, order, persuade, remind, teach, tell.*

> Peter advised Ron **to call the police**.
> Esther reminded her teacher **to assign some homework**.

Verbs that can be followed either directly by the *to* **infinitive** or by an **object** + the *to* **infinitive** include: *ask, expect, help, intend, like, love, hate, mean, prefer, want, wish.*

> I certainly intended **to go** to the party.
> We really expected **Samantha to pass** the exam.

> Note this difference:
> I want **to have** a cat = It will be my cat.
> I want **her to have** a cat = It will be her cat.
> Dad likes **to wash** the car = Dad washes the car.
> Dad likes **John to wash** the car = John washes the car.

Verbs followed by the *-ing* form include: *avoid, be used to, delay, dislike, escape, finish, forgive, give up, go on, imagine.*

> I usually **avoid going** into town late at night.
> Miriam **hates peeling** potatoes.
> Have you **finished reading** that book yet?

- Some verbs may be followed either by the **to** infinitive or by the **-ing** form with little or no change in meaning. These verbs include: *begin, start, cease, continue, intend, like, love, hate, prefer.*

    > He began **to run** around.
    > He began **running** around.
    > She likes **to swim** in the sea.
    > She likes **swimming** in the sea.
    > I can't bear **to see** violence.
    > I can't bear **seeing** violence.

- Some verbs may be followed either by the **to** infinitive or by the **-ing** form but the meaning of the sentence changes depending on the form that is used. These verbs include: *try, forget, remember.*

    > I **remembered to turn** the lights off before we went out. = I turned the lights off.
    > I **remember turning** the lights off before we went out. = I specifically remember doing this.

    > She **tried to talk** to him, but his secretary wouldn't put the call through.
    > She **tried talking** to him, but he wouldn't listen.

Particularly after verbs such as go and come, the to infinitive is understood to express purpose.

    > She has **gone to do** the shopping.
    > They **came** here **to learn** English.

Use of the verb followed by the **-ing** form concentrates on what happens. The second verb is really the object of the first one. These verbs include: *remember, forget, try.*

    > I definitely **remember switching the lights off** *before we went out.*
    > She **tried talking to him,** *but he wouldn't listen.*

Some **set expressions** (idioms) are followed by an *-ing* form.
These include: *it's not worth*, and *it's no fun*.

> It's **no fun going** out alone.
> It's **no use phoning** him; he's gone away.
> It's **worth trying** one more time.

The noun phrase

A noun phrase is a word or group of words that can function as the
subject, the **object**, or the **complement** in a sentence.

> *The manager interviewed all the applicants on Tuesday.*
> *Lydia was the successful applicant.*

See pp. 18–19 and pp. 229–230 for more information about these
functions. A noun phrase must always contain a noun or a pronoun.

A noun phrase may consist of only one word. That word will be either
a noun or a pronoun.

> *Mary left late.*
> *She left late.*
> *Cheese is expensive.*
> *It is expensive.*

A noun phrase may consist of more than one word. One of these words,
a noun or a pronoun, is the **headword** in the phrase. The other words
describe or modify the headword.

> *the tall girl*
> *the very tall girl*
> *a strikingly beautiful girl*
> *the tall girl with green eyes*

Words that go before the headword are called **premodifiers**. A noun
can be premodified by:

– a determiner. See p. 160.

> *the girl*   *that boy*
> *a spider*   *some rice*

- one or more adjectives. See pp. 160–190.

   tall girls
   tall dark girls
   tall dark handsome men

- a number, another noun, or the present participle or past participle of a verb.

   three days
   the *bus station* cafeteria
   an *annoying* habit
   an *overworked* man

Words that go after the headword are called **postmodifiers**. A noun can be postmodified by:

- a prepositional phrase (a noun phrase with a preposition in front of it).

   the person *in the corner*
   the view *across the valley*
   the house *beside the church*
   creatures *under the sea*

- a subordinate clause (usually one beginning with *who*, *which* or *that*). See p. 263.

   All the women *who had gathered there* finally went away.
   Milk *that has been kept too long* can go sour.

- less commonly, certain adjectives. See p. 160.

   an attorney *general*
   peaches *galore*
   the president *elect*

- Personal pronouns are only rarely premodified or postmodified. See p. 202.

    Silly me.
    Poor old you.

Types of noun

Nouns can be classified according to what they refer to.

- Nouns that are really names are called **proper nouns**. Proper nouns usually refer to a particular named person, place, or thing.

They include:

– the names of specific people.

Mohammed Belhaus   *John Lennon*
Takisha Everett   *Mrs. Merton*

– geographical items.

Spain   *Mount Everest*
China   *Alaska*
the Rio Grande   *Calgary*
Madison Square Garden   *Sunset Boulevard*

– days of the week, months, and annual Church festivals.

Thursday   *June*
Christmas   *Easter*

– patented products and company names.

Prozac   *Tide*
Toyota   *Samsung*

– newspaper and magazine titles.

The New York Times   *Vogue*
Science News   *Wired*

— stores, stadiums, theaters, buildings.

> *The Majestic*   *Macy's*
> *Wrigley Field*   *The Chrysler Building*

— titles (the polite or professional labels that we give to people).

> **Doctor** *Mahajan*   **Sir** *Elton John*
> **Professor** *James*   **President** *Sarkozy*

A person's title is usually placed before his or her name. Proper nouns and titles are always written with an initial capital letter.

● All the other nouns that refer to things or species are called **common nouns**.

> I put the **tennis balls** in that **basket** there.
> My **brother** and **sister** visited my **mother**.
> The **anger** that John felt was overwhelming.

Common nouns can be divided into the following groups, according to their meaning:

Abstract nouns. These refer to intangible items (that is, things that are not physical objects).

> *honesty*   *anger*
> *idea*   *time*
> *ugliness*   *behavior*

Concrete nouns. These refer to tangible items (that is, physical objects).

> *pig*   *granite*
> *table*   *farmer*
> *brother*   *sugar*

A concrete noun may refer to a living thing (**animate** nouns) or a physical object (**inanimate** nouns).

Collective nouns. These refer to collections of people or animals.

> *a **herd** of cows*
> *a **swarm** of bees*

Nouns may also be classified according to the words that they are used with, that is:

– whether or not the noun gives us information about **singular** and **plural number**.

– the other words that can be used in the same noun phrase.

This gives us a useful distinction between **countable nouns** and **uncountable nouns**.

Countable nouns refer to things that we can count: *one cat*, *two cats*, *seventeen cats*, and so on. They have singular and plural forms. They must be used with a determiner if they are singular.

> ***Dogs** ran wild in the streets.*
> ***The dog** is loose again.*
> *Bring **a chair** for Mandy, will you?*
> *We've bought **six new chairs**.*

Uncountable nouns refer to:

– things that are not normally thought of as countable.

> *John asked me for some **advice**.*
> *Anna gave us some more **information** about her **work**.*
> ***Homework** occupied much of Sonia's evening.*

–   qualities or abstract ideas.

> *Our **knowledge** of outer **space** is increasing daily.*
> *Troy gave **evidence** at the trial.*
> ***Anger** is a normal human emotion.*

Uncountable nouns do not usually have a plural form. They are followed by a singular verb. They are not normally used with the indefinite article. (You cannot talk about "*an advice*" or "*a money*.") When it is necessary to think of an item as countable it has to be used with a **partitive noun**. See p. 141.

> *He bought seven **yards of** cloth.*
> *Let me give you **a piece of** advice.*

Some of the commonest uncountable nouns are: *advice, anger, beauty, behavior, conduct, education, evidence, furniture, happiness, information, knowledge, leisure, management, money, news, power, progress, research, safety, work.*

●   Verbal nouns, sometimes called gerunds (p. 158), which are formed from the present participle of verbs, can also be used as uncountable nouns.

> *Why don't you try **walking** to work?*
> *Brian was trying to stop **smoking**.*
> *The **ringing** in his ears continued.*

Note that nouns that are uncountable in English may be countable in other languages. See p. 142.

Mass nouns

Mass nouns refer to a substance that can be divided or measured but not counted, e.g., *sugar*, *water*. They do not usually have an indefinite article in front.

> **Meat** *is often less expensive than* **cheese**.
> **Sugar** *is quite cheap*.

Mass nouns only take a plural in special cases. They can be counted when they refer to:

– a particular type or types of the substance.

> *There was a buffet of bread and rolls, cheese,* **cold meats**,
> *and tea or coffee.*
> *Rosa brought out a tempting selection of* **French cheeses**.
> **The principal sugars** *are glucose, sucrose, and fructose.*

– a serving of the substance.

> **Two sodas**, *please*.
> *He went up to the bar and ordered* **two beers**.

• Mass nouns are often used together with a partitive noun.

> *There are only* **two pieces of furniture** *in the room.*
> *There are* **three portions of meat** *in this package.*
> **Five pitchers of beer**, *please*.

Partitive nouns

Partitive nouns, sometimes just called partitives, are commonly
followed by *of*. They are used when we need to talk about a part of a
mass noun or when we need to count the quantity of something that is
referred to by an uncountable noun or a mass noun, especially when it
is necessary to talk about:

– measurements and quantities with mass nouns.

> *three **pieces** of toast*   *a **slice** of cheese*
> *a **bit** of fluff*   *two **spoonfuls** of sugar*

– individual items with uncountable nouns.

> *Two **pieces** of furniture needed major repairs.*
> *We needed several **lengths** of string.*

– a collection of countable nouns.

> *The road was blocked by a **flock** of sheep.*
> *He has a small **herd** of dairy cows.*
> *There was a **crowd** of football fans on the bus.*
> *A **couple** of cats were fighting.*

> Many collective nouns can be used as partitive nouns.
> See p. 138.

Nouns that have both countable and uncountable uses

Most nouns are either countable or uncountable, as explained on p. 138. Some nouns, however, behave like countable nouns in some sentences and uncountable nouns in other sentences. They usually have different meanings depending on how they are used. For example, *time*, *light*, *history*, *space*, *laugh*, and *service* have more than one meaning.

> *Time passed slowly.*
> *She did it four times.*
> *Light travels faster than sound.*
> *The lights in this room are too bright.*
> *The rocket was launched into space.*
> *How many spaces are left in the parking lot?*

Some nouns that are countable nouns in other languages are used only as uncountable nouns in English, e.g., *help*, *information*, *advice*.

> *He received all the necessary information.*
> *I don't need your help.*

Some nouns are used only in the plural form, even when we are talking about one item, e.g., *pants*, *clothes*, *jeans*. We can use a partitive noun with *of* when referring to a single item.

> *These slacks need cleaning.*
> *Put the scissors back when you have finished with them.*
> *I need a pair of pliers.*
> *Liz gathered up a bundle of clothes.*

Gender of nouns

In some languages, nouns have **gender**. This means that a noun causes other words such as adjectives to change their spelling according to certain rules. Grammatical gender often has no relationship with biological gender. English does not have **grammatical gender** for nouns.

On the other hand, the biological gender of the thing or person referred to does affect a few areas of English grammar.

> *a cow... **she** or it*   *a bull... **he** or it*
> *a girl... **she***   *a boy... **he***

Gender distinctions are relevant where personal pronouns (p. 202) and possessive determiners (p. 160) have to be decided on. These distinctions are only noticeable in **singular** nouns.

> ***He** found **his** book.*
> ***He** had been looking for **it**.*
> ***She** found **her** book.*
> ***She** had been looking for **it**.*

There are also special cases, such as the association of neuter gender with babies and small animals, or feminine gender with a vehicle.

> *I just saw a **mouse**. **It** was running across the room.*
> *The **spider** was spinning **its** web.*
> *The **beetle** crawled into **its** hole.*
> *The **baby** threw down **its** rattle.*
> *I've got a new boat; **she's** a real beauty.*

Nouns denoting male persons and animals are **masculine**. They are used with the pronouns and possessive determiners *he, him, his*.

Nouns denoting female persons and animals are **feminine**. They are used with the pronouns and possessive determiners *she, her, hers*.

*Barry saw Linda. **He** called out to **her** that **he** had found **her** book.*
*Marcia saw Paul. **She** called out to **him** that **she** had found **his** book.*
*Madeleine saw Kim. **She** said "Hello" to **her**.*

The pronouns and possessive determiners used to refer to common or **neuter** nouns are *it* and *its*.

***The truth** will emerge. **It** always does.*

Nouns denoting inanimate objects and abstract notions are also neuter and are referred to with *it* and *its*.

- Some nouns denoting people have the same form for masculine and feminine. Nouns used for a group, e.g., *government* or *team*, have **common** or **neuter** gender, even when we know that the group is made up exclusively of male or female members.

    *The **government** has changed **its** policy.*
    *The **team** has won **its** first medal at a major championship.*

With some nouns of common gender it might be possible to specify the gender if we had enough information. But if we do not have this knowledge, the choice of pronoun or possessive determiner becomes a problem.

    a driver...he/she
    the cook...he/she
    doctor...he/she

As a way around this problem, in informal and spoken English, **their** is sometimes used after a singular noun or an indefinite pronoun.
See p. 201. Many people consider this grammatically unacceptable, but it is widely used to avoid repetitions of *his* or *her* or *him* or *her*.

    *Each **student** must apply to **his or her** tutor for an extension.*
    *Everyone must apply to **their** tutor for an extension.*
    *Someone has left **their** coat in my room.*

The specialized terms used to name male, female and neutered animals show a number of gender differences.

any animal	fertile female	fertile male	infertile male
horse	mare	stallion	gelding
–	cow	bull	steer
sheep	ewe	ram	wether

Gender differences are also shown in the nouns that indicate relationships.

parent	mother	father
child	daughter	son

- Many nouns denoting an occupation have no explicit gender.

engineer	doctor	programmer
mechanic	lawyer	driver

Some occupations and professions have a special feminine form for the noun.

> Call your branch **manager** today.
> Sue is **manageress** of a hairdressing salon.
> **Authors** from all over the state attended the ceremony.
> Here in the studio to talk about her new book is **authoress** Mary Farrell.

Many people prefer to avoid these forms, regarding the distinction as unnecessary.

> Anne Tyler is a highly successful **author**.
> Meryl Streep is one of our finest **actors**.
> Michelle Stewart has been promoted to Office **Manager**.

Some speakers prefer to use a different form of the word or an entirely different word in order to avoid a gender-marked noun.

the chairman   *the chairperson*   *the chair*

Many speakers use newer terms with a single name for professions or jobs that formerly used different terms for male and female.

steward	*stewardess*	*flight attendant*
mailman	*mailwoman*	*letter carrier*
waiter	*waitress*	*server*

If necessary, the gender of a common noun can be made clear by adding a descriptive term such as *woman* or *male/female*.

*Would you prefer to see **a woman doctor**?*
***Male employees** should use locker room B.*

If we are discussing a country from an emotional, economic, or political viewpoint we sometimes use feminine gender.

*Poland has made steady progress restructuring **her** economy.*

Showing possession through nouns

Possession can be shown in three ways:

– by using a possessive pronoun that refers to an earlier noun.

> The **man** was repairing **his** car.
> The **students** received **their** grades today.

– by adding -'s to a singular noun, or an irregular plural noun that does not end in -s.

> one dog   one boy   several children
> the **dog's** bones   the **boy's** books   the **children's** toys

– by adding -' to a plural noun.

> more than one dog   more than one boy
> the **dogs'** bones   the **boys'** books

There is also the **of possessive** (a noun phrase with **of** followed by another noun).

> the side **of the** ship   the end **of the** line

The **of possessive** is not just a different way of saying the same thing as the -'s possessive.

> the **boy's** pencil   **but not** the pencil of the boy

The -'s possessive is generally used only with nouns referring to tangible items and in time phrases.

> the **driver's** foot   the **dog's** nose
> the **woman's** house   the **company's** logo
> **today's** newspaper   a **week's** vacation

The *of* possessive is generally used with nouns referring to inanimate things (i.e., objects) and abstract ideas.

> the leg *of* the table   the arm *of* the sofa
> the wheel *of* the car   the foot *of* the bed
> the world *of* ideas   the power *of* thought

The function of the possessive form in English is to:

– show possession.

> the **boy's** books   the **dog's** blanket

– show a relationship, with a person either as the originator, or the user of the thing named.

> her **parents'** consent   the **student's** letter
> a **women's** club   the **children's** park

– indicate that a place is where someone lives.

> the **Feezers'**   my **aunt's**

– show that something is a part of a whole.

> the leg *of* the table   the **dog's** nose
> the wheel *of* the car   the **girl's** shoulder

– add a descriptive element that premodifies a noun. It is a type of determiner. See also p. 160.

> **writer's** cramp   A *Winter's* Tale

Rules for the formation of the possessive -*'s* (apostrophe -*s*) and -*s'* (-*s* apostrophe) are as follows:

– most singular nouns add an apostrophe + -s.

> *a **girl's** ring*   *a **cat's** face*

– most plural nouns add an apostrophe after the plural form -s.

> *the **boys'** football*   *five young **girls'** faces*

There are exceptions for the following:

– common nouns that end in -s in the singular. When these are made plural the choice of -'s or a simple apostrophe is optional.

> *a cactus*   *the **cactus'** spines*   *the **cactus's** habitat*

– plural nouns not ending in -s, such as those that have a plural ending in -*en*. In this case, add an apostrophe + s.

> ***children's***   ***men's***

– proper nouns and common nouns that end in -s. These usually add -'s in the singular unless the final sound of the basic word is [-iz], in which case, a simple apostrophe is enough.

> *Mrs. **Evans's** car*   *Mr. **Jones's** fence*
> ***Keats's** poetry*   *the **Bates's** cat*
> ***Dickens's** novels*   *Peter **Bridges'** car*

Compound nouns (see p. 151) put the -'s or the simple apostrophe at the end of the complete compound.

> *my mother-in-law*   *my **mother-in-law's** car*
> *the runner-up*   *the **runner-up's** trophy*
> *the fact-checkers*   *the **fact-checkers'** questions*

Noun phrases that are descriptive of someone's role or profession put the -'s on the headword of the phrase.

> *a stock market analyst's annual income*
> *the senior food inspector's monthly visit*

If they use an of construction the -'s or simple apostrophe usually goes on the last noun.

> *the governor of Iowa's official car*
> *the director of marketing's personal assistant*

Compound nouns

A compound noun is a noun that is formed from two or more words. The meaning of the whole compound is often different from the meaning of the two words on their own. Compound nouns are very common. The main noun is normally the last one.

teapot	*headache*
*washing **machine***	*liquor **license***
self-control	*C-note*

Compound nouns are commonly formed from the following word combinations:

- noun + noun
- verb + noun
- adjective + noun
- phrasal verb used as noun
- particle + noun

noun + noun:	*boyfriend*	*skinhead*
verb + noun:	*breakfast*	*grindstone*
adjective + noun:	*software*	*hardware*
phrasal verb:	*a break-in*	*a take-over*
particle + noun:	*onlooker*	*aftershave*

The term **particle** is used here for a word that can be either an adverb or a preposition.

Compound nouns can be written:

– as one word.

> bookcase   wallpaper
> birdcage   snowflake

– as two words.

> post office   fire engine
> eye shadow   cough drop

– with a hyphen.

> anti-Zionist   air-conditioning
> all-nighter   T-shirt

Consult a dictionary to discover how the word is normally written. There are often alternative forms to be found, for example, *drop down menu*, *drop-down menu*, and *dropdown menu* are all currently acceptable forms of the same compound noun.

Nouns as modifiers

The compound noun *girlfriend* names a special sort of *friend*. Nouns can also be used as **modifiers** without forming a compound noun.

> a **concrete** slab   old **oak** beams
> an **auto** mechanic   a **store** manager

A noun that is used as a modifier has the same function as an adjective. The first noun usually makes the second one more specific, but we do not think of it as part of a combination that forms a new word. See p. 186 for more on modifiers.

Number in nouns

Singular number is used when the noun refers to one item.
Plural number is used when the noun refers to more than one item.

Countable nouns have both singular and plural forms.

Uncountable nouns and **mass nouns** do not normally have a plural form. See p. 136 for more on the types of noun.

The regular plural ending of an English noun is -s.

cat   *cats*

These are the exceptions to the normal pattern:

singular noun ending	plural noun ending
-s, -ss, -ch, -x, -zz	-es
focus	focuses
princess	princesses
church	churches
box	boxes
buzz	buzzes
-o	-s or -es
hero	heroes
taco	tacos
piano	pianos
potato	potatoes
consonant + y	-ies
baby	babies
hobby	hobbies
vowel + y	-s
key	keys
ray	rays

singular noun ending	plural noun ending
-f hoof dwarf thief roof	–s or –ves hoofs or hooves dwarfs or dwarves thieves roofs
-fe knife life	-ves knives lives

Irregular plurals

Some nouns have two plural forms.

fish   fish or fishes

Some of them have the same form in the singular and plural.

a sheep   ten sheep
a deer   seven deer

A few change a vowel to form the plural.

man   men
woman   women
foot   feet
mouse   mice

Some nouns form the plural with *-en*.

child   children
ox   oxen

Since it is not possible to give more than a selection of the irregular forms, you should check in a dictionary if you are unsure about a plural form. If the dictionary does not show the plural form, then you can assume that it is regular.

Compound nouns normally form the plural by adding *-s* to the last word of the compound.

a game console	*three game consoles*
a bookcase	*two bookcases*
a Mexican take-away	*two Mexican take-aways*

There are a few exceptions:

A compound noun formed from a noun and an adverb often makes the first word plural. However, a few of these plurals are formed regularly.

a passer-by	*several* **passers-by**
a hanger-on	*several* **hangers-on**
a break-in	*several* **break-ins**
a play-off	*several* **play-offs**

Compound nouns with *woman* as the first word make both words plural.

a woman doctor	*several* **women** *doctors*
a woman driver	*most* **women** *drivers*

A compound word which ends in *-ful* normally adds *-s* after *-ful*, but there is an alternative form with the *-s* following the base noun.

a cupful	*three* **cupfuls/cupsful**
a spoonful	*two* **spoonfuls/spoonsful**

Plural nouns with singular reference

Some nouns referring to clothes and tools where two equal parts are joined together, e.g., *pants*, *binoculars*, and *tongs*, are treated as being plural and are followed by a verb in the plural.

> My shorts **are** dirty.
> The scissors **are** on the table.

To talk about one of these items we can use the expression *a pair of...*

> John bought **a pair of** jeans.

To talk about more than one we talk about however many *pairs of...*

> Martina bought **five pairs of** tights.

- When they are used as ordinary numbers, words such as *dozen* and *million* have no plural form.

> **nine million** stars   **two dozen** glasses

When they are used to mean a large number, they do have a plural form, which can be used as a partitive.

> There are **millions** of pebbles on the beach.
> I saw **dozens** of children in the park.

Foreign plurals

Nouns that have come into English from foreign languages can:

- keep the plural form of the language they come from.

> an axis   two axes
> a phenomenon   two phenomena

– have plurals formed according to the rules for plural in English.

    a thesaurus   *several thesauruses*
                                      (instead of thesauri)

– have two plurals: one from the foreign language and the other formed according to the rules for plural formation in English. The foreign plural is usually kept for scientific or specialized use.

    an index   *some indexes/indices*
    a formula   *some formulas/formulae*

Verbal nouns

A **verbal noun** is the -*ing* form, i.e., the present participle of the verb, used as a noun. It can be used in all the places that a noun can be used, but still keeps some characteristics of the verb. It is sometimes called a **gerund**.

> The **screaming** of the brakes terrified me.
> **Smoking** is prohibited.

The verbal noun normally functions as an uncountable noun, as above. However, there are some uses of the verbal noun that can be preceded by an indefinite article or used in the plural.

> He gave **a reading** from his latest volume of poetry.
> The movie was shot with alternative **endings**.

The verbal noun can be preceded by the definite article, by adjectives, and by possessives.

> Her fantastic **singing** won Helen the scholarship.

Just like any noun, the verbal noun can function:

– as a **subject**.

> **Driving** was impossible.

– as the **complement** of the verb *be*.

> **Seeing** is **believing**.
> His greatest pleasure is **working**.

– as an **object** after certain verbs. See also p. 130.

> Louisa likes **swimming** but Helen prefers **diving**.

– after **prepositions** to make a prepositional phrase.

> *Can you watch them **without laughing**?*

Verbal nouns are also used:

– after some phrasal verbs such as: *be for/against, give up, keep on, look forward to, put off*. See also page 139.

> *She was all for **leaving** immediately.*
> *Linda gave up **swimming** but she kept on **dieting**.*
> *They were looking forward to **writing** home.*

– after certain set expressions such as: *can't stand, can't help, it's no use/good*.

> *I can't stand **waiting** around.*
> *I can't help **getting** upset.*
> *It's no use **crying** over spilled milk.*

The **possessive determiner** can be used with the verbal noun, especially in formal English.

> *Anna left the house without **my knowing**.*

● The verbal noun also has:

– a perfect form: *having ...ed*.

> *Martin was accused of **having cheated**.*

– a passive form: *being ...ed*.

> ***Being asked** did not bother me.*

– a perfect passive form: *having been ...ed*.

> *The car showed no sign of **having been touched**.*

Determiners

Determiners are words that make the reference of nouns more specific. If I say "*this car*" it is clear that I mean a particular car that is near me. If I change it to "*my car*" I am saying something specific about ownership.

Determiners can be divided into several kinds according to:

– their meaning.

– what they may go with and where they may come in the noun phrase.

There are eight classes of determiner:

– the indefinite article *a* or *an*. See p. 162.

> *A man came into the shop.*
> *An honest person would return the car to the owner.*

– the definite article *the*. See p. 164.

> *The dog chased the rabbit.*

– the demonstratives *this*, *that*, *these*, *those*. See p. 168.

> *This book is better than that one.*
> *These apples are redder than those ones.*

– the possessives *my*, *your*, *his*, *her*, *its*, *our*, *their*. See p. 207.

> *I gave my share to her sister.*
> *Shirona found his book in her car.*

– the quantifiers *some*, *any*, *enough*, *no*, *all*, *both*, *half*, *double*, *several*, *much*, *many*, *more*, *most*, *few*, *fewer*, *fewest*, *a few*, *little* (meaning not much), *less*, *least*, *a little*. See pp. 171–177.

> I've got **some** coffee but I haven't got **any** sugar.
> Have you got **much** money on you?
> There were **no** witnesses to the accident.
> **Both** girls saw the attack.
> **Few** people know the answer to that.
> The safety net gives **little** help to those who need it most.

– the numbers, cardinal (*one*, *two*, *three*...), and ordinal (*first*, *second*, *third*...). See p. 176.

> There's **one** thing I need to ask you.
> The **two** boys grew up together in Manhattan.
> **Three** men were found hiding in the building.
> Their **second** child is due in October.
> She lost in the **third** round of the tournament.

– the distributives *each*, *every*, *either*, *neither*. See p. 178.

> **Each** child received a book.
> **Every** girl was given a number to wear.
> **Either** book should help you with the problem.

– the exclamatives *what*, *such*. See p. 180.

> **What** nonsense!
> **What** a shame!
> They make **such** a fuss over small things!

Generally, a noun phrase has only one determiner in it, or none at all. A few determiners, e.g., *all*, *both*, and the numbers, can be used together with another determiner. See p. 160.

The indefinite article

The indefinite article is *a* or *an*. The form *an* is used before a word that starts with a vowel sound.

> *a girl*   *a cat*
> *an eight-year-old girl*   *an honor*

The indefinite article is used with singular countable nouns:

− to refer to a person or a thing that you are mentioning for the first time in a conversation or a piece of writing.

> *A man was seen driving away in a black car.*

− to refer to a person or a thing that you do not want to be specific about.

> *I stopped off at a kiosk to buy a newspaper.*
> *You go past a gas station on the left, and then you'll see our street on the right.*

− to refer to a person or a thing that you cannot be more specific about because there is not enough information.

> *A man came by to see you this afternoon.*
> *There was a telephone call for you a minute ago.*

− in definitions.

> *An octopus is a sea creature with eight tentacles.*

− when you refer to a person's profession.

> *Her father is a dentist and her mother is a teacher.*

- to express the quantity *one*. If you wish to emphasize this quantity, then use *one* instead of the indefinite article. The equivalent for plural nouns is *some* or no determiner at all. See p. 160.

> *I want a needle and a thimble.*
> *Would you like a glass of wine?*
> *There is only **one** glass of wine left in the bottle.*
> *Guy has bought a skateboard.*
> *We've got three pairs of rollerblades and **one** skateboard.*

It is the sound, not the spelling, that decides where *an* is used. For example, although *unique* begins with a vowel, the sound at the beginning resembles a *y-* sound. *Honest*, by contrast, begins with a silent consonant and a vowel sound.

> *an idiot*   *an honest mistake*
> *a unicorn*   *a unique experience*

> There are a few words that begin with a silent *h-*, in front of which *an* should be used. They are: *heir, herb* (for some speakers), *heiress, hombre, honest, honor, hors d'oeuvre, hour.*

- Very formal or old-fashioned speakers also use the *an* form with some words beginning with an *h-* that is not silent, especially *historical* and *hotel*.

> *I waited **an** hour.*
> *They joined a historical society.*
> *They joined **an** historical society.*   *(old-fashioned English)*
> *They were staying at a hotel.*
> *They were staying at **an** hotel.*   *(old-fashioned English)*

The definite article

The definite article is *the*.

The definite article is used with singular and plural nouns. It is used both with countable nouns and uncountable nouns:

– to make definite or specific reference to a person or a thing that has already been referred to.

> *There's **the** man I was telling you about!*

– to refer to a person or thing that is already specific because those listening or reading know what you are talking about. In the first example below, "*the children*" would be members of our family and "*the swimming pool*" is the swimming pool we normally go to.

> *Let's take **the** children to **the** swimming pool.*
> *Did you switch **the** heating on?*
> *There were drinks in **the** fridge but **the** beer was soon finished.*

– to generalize about a whole class or species, usually of plants or animals. A singular noun is used for this purpose. The first example means "*The elephant species is still hunted for its tusks.*"

> ***The** elephant is still hunted for its tusks.*
> ***The** snowdrop is the first flower to arrive in the new year.*

– when it is followed by an adjective used as a noun indicating nationality, or when generalizing about a whole class of people. *The Dutch* in the first example means "*Dutch people in general.*"

> ***The** Dutch are very skillful engineers.*
> ***The** poor were crowding the streets of the capital.*
> ***The** homeless were sheltered in the church.*

– before the names of rivers, groups of islands, seas, oceans, and mountain ranges.

The Ohio
The Caribbean Sea

The Aleutians
The Pacific

– before the names of certain public institutions, most newspapers, and some magazines.

The Whitney Museum
The Lyceum Theater
The Washington Post
The Economist

The Hilton Hotel
The Capitol
The LA Times
The New England Journal of Medicine

– before the names of well-known institutions, even when a specific one is not named—usually because it is not important to know which one is meant.

> An ambulance took her to **the hospital**.
> His mom had to pick him up at **the police station**.
> They like to walk their dogs in **the park**.

– before parts of the body when these are referred to in an impersonal way.

> A stone struck him on **the hand**.
> Martin hit him on **the head**.

• The definite article is rarely used with titles when they are followed by a name. Proper nouns that refer to persons, such as *Sue* and *Ron*, and proper nouns used in conjunction with titles, such as *Queen Elizabeth*, *Doctor Thomas*, and *Captain Parry*, only take a definite article if:

– they stand for the name of a thing such as a boat.

> **The Queen Elizabeth II** *is on a long cruise.*

– a distinction is being made between people who have identical names. This use can give emphasis to the noun.

> Ah, no. **The David Parry I know** lives in Minnesota.
> I saw Paul Kay in town this morning. – Not **the** Paul Kay?

Nouns used without a determiner

Certain noun phrases do not have a determiner at all.

We usually leave out the determiner when we use a noun or a noun phrase in the plural to make a generalization.

> He sells **cars** for a living.
> **Tigers** are nearing extinction.
> **Onions** are good for you.
> **Grassy hills** rise on all sides of the town.

Singular nouns that are uncountable (including mass nouns) are used without a determiner when you are making a general reference.

> New **information** is now available.
> Do you like **jelly**?
> This shop sells **furniture**.

● This is particularly true when the uncountable noun is used for the first time in a general way in the course of a conversation or piece of writing. They can be used with a determiner when the reference becomes specific. For example, you can ask someone if they like *cake* as a rule, and then ask the person if she would like some of *your cake*.

> **The** information she gave me was inaccurate.
> Would you like some of **the cake** I made for the party?
> We don't let the dog climb onto **the** furniture.

There are a number of idiomatic expressions that usually omit a determiner. Examples are expressions that refer to:

– travel, when you proceed **by**: *bicycle, car, bus, train, ship, boat, plane, subway*.

> Anna went **by bicycle** but Lucy went **by taxi**.
> He was chased by police **on foot**.

– specific times (or events connected with them) with the prepositions *at*, *before*, or *by*, *dawn*, *sunrise*, *sunset*, *noon*, *midnight*, *night*, *breakfast*, *supper*, *dinner*, *day*, *night*.

> Tomoko rose **at dawn** and went to bed **at sunset**.
> We swam in the pool **by day** and partied **by night**.

– meals: to have *breakfast*, *lunch*, *brunch*, *supper*, *dinner*.

> Jane had **breakfast** at home.
> She met Diana **for lunch**.

– some institutions, with the prepositions *in*, *to*, *at*, or sometimes *from*: *church*, *college*, *jail*, *prison*, *school*, *work*.

> John went **to college** in Wisconsin.
> Luella was sent home **from school** today.
> Ruth was **at home** all day.

– seasons of the year, when you are generalizing, e.g.: *in spring*, *in summer*, *in autumn*, *in winter*. With *fall*, however, the definite article is usually used.

> **In spring**, the potatoes are planted by machine.
> The place is packed **in summer**.
> **In the fall**, the grapes are harvested by hand.

However, all of these words are used with the definite article when you are talking about a specific time, place, season, etc.

> Philip traveled by **the same train** as Mehandra.
> Just look at **the wonderful sunset**.
> Pam works at **the prison**.
> I can't work well **in the summer**.

Demonstratives

Demonstratives are used to specify the distance of something in space or time in relation to the speaker.

The **demonstratives** are: *this*, *that*, *these*, *those*.

This and *these* refer to objects near the speaker.

> *This apple looks ripe.*
> *These apples come from Oregon.*

The reference may be nearness in time, especially future time.

> *I'll stop by this afternoon.*
> *The festival ends this Thursday.*
> *This summer is the warmest I can remember.*

That and *those* refer to objects that are further away from the speaker.

> *I think that boy over there is lost.*
> *Can you see those people up on the hill?*

This and *that* are used before singular countable nouns and uncountable nouns.

> *I can take down this painting, but I can't reach that one.*
> *This book is mine, but that magazine isn't.*

These and *those* are used before plural countable nouns.

> *I'm peeling these potatoes to make hash browns.*
> *Those men are repairing the roof.*

Possessives

Possessives are used to specify the ownership of an item, or, if the noun refers to something living, to specify a relationship.

> That is **my car**.
> Mr. Smith was **my teacher** in sixth grade.

The form of the possessive changes according to the number and gender of the person or thing that possesses the item.

> **His brothers** all came to the wedding.
> **Their aunt** lives in St. Louis, but **their cousins** live in Chicago.
> **Your shoes** are under **your bed**.

person	singular	plural
1st	*my*	*our*
2nd	*your*	*your*
3rd *(masculine)*	*his*	*their*
3rd *(feminine)*	*her*	*their*
3rd *(neuter)*	*its*	*their*

> Possessive determiners, which can go into a noun phrase, are not the same as possessive pronouns (*mine*, *hers*, *yours*, etc.), which can stand alone. See p. 144.

Another sort of possessive is the **possessive phrase**. This acts just like a possessive word but is a noun or noun phrase ending in -'s or -s'. A possessive phrase acts as a possessive determiner, but may itself include one of the other determiners.

Robert's mother
the visitors' restroom
a good day's work
the President's press secretary

Sally's new job
the residents' dining room
my wife's cousin

Quantifiers

Quantifiers are used to indicate the amount or quantity of something referred to by a noun. They are different from numbers because they indicate an approximate amount rather than an exact amount. They can be grouped according to their use.

all, some, any, much, enough, no

– You can use *all*, *some*, *any*, or *enough* before a plural countable noun or an uncountable noun.

> Can I have **some** chips, please?
> Anna gave me **all** her money.
> Peter never has **any** time to visit us.

You can use *no* before a singular or a plural countable noun or an uncountable noun.

> There were **no** pictures of the party.
> There is **no** hospital in this town.
> **No** information has been released yet.

– *Some*, *any*, *much*, and *enough* are used to refer to a part of the item.

> Would you like **some** ice cream?
> We didn't have **much** success.
> I haven't seen **enough** evidence to convince me.
> I couldn't find **any** fresh eggs at the supermarket.

All and *no* refer to the whole of the item.

> **All the milk** has been used.
> There is **no milk** in the fridge.

- *Some* is used in positive sentences.

   > I've bought **some** chocolate.
   > I found **some** great deals in town this morning.

- *Any* is used in negative sentences.

   > I didn't buy **any** chocolate this week.
   > I haven't seen **any** birds in the backyard today.

- In questions, *any* is used when there is no particular expectation about the answer; *some* is used when the answer is expected to be positive.

   > Have you got **any** double-A batteries?
   > Has Paul heard **any** news about the accident?
   > Would you like **some** cake, Aisha?

- The use of *no* with *there is/are* is very common.

   > There was **no mail** today.
   > There are **no jobs** available for electricians at the moment.

half, double, both

- *Half* can be used with countable nouns and with uncountable nouns.

   > **Half the time** I didn't understand what was going on.
   > **Half the students** came from overseas.

- *Double* is used with uncountable nouns.

   > We're going to need **double the present supply** of water.
   > They want **double the money** they originally asked for.

– **Both** is used to define two things represented by a plural countable noun.

> **Both men** were given another chance.
> **Both dogs** had to be put down.

See p. 161 for more information about quantifiers when they are used with other determiners.

The following quantifiers are used to express **graded** amounts of an item (i.e., whether there is more or less of something).

> Have you seen **many tourists** in town?
> Yes, I've seen **more tourists** than usual.
> I think **most tourists** just stay for a couple of days.
>
> I didn't put **much gas** in the car.
> I think we need **more gas**.
> The news caused **much excitement**.
> **Most information** about our services is available on the Internet.

– **Many**, **more**, **most** are used with graded quantities of plural countable nouns.

> Have you seen **many tourists** in town?
> Yes, I've seen **more tourists** than usual.
> I think **most tourists** just stay for a couple of days.

– **Much**, **more**, **most** are used with graded quantities of uncountable nouns.

> I didn't put **much gas** in the car.
> I think we need **more gas**.
> The news caused **much excitement**.
> **Most information** about our services is available on the Internet.

— *Few, fewer, fewest* are used with graded quantities of plural countable nouns.

> *Few people know the answer to this problem.*
> *Fewer loans are being granted than usual.*
> *Japanese workers take the fewest holidays.*

— *Little, less, least* are used with graded quantities of uncountable nouns.

> *There is little chance of rain today.*
> *This technique causes less harm to the environment.*
> *I need to get from one place to another with the least inconvenience.*

Many speakers do not make the above distinction and use less and least with both countable and uncountable nouns. This is common but not technically correct.

● *A few*, and *a little* are different from *few* and *little* on their own because they have a positive sense. *Few* means "not many":

> *Few buildings survived the earthquake.*

but *a few* means "several."

> *A few kind people helped the injured man.*
> *A few delays are inevitable.*

Little means "not much":

> *The students were given very little help with their projects.*
> *Edward got little encouragement from his parents.*

but *a little* means "some."

> I need *a little help* from my friends.
> Everyone needs *a little encouragement* now and then.
> Do you take sugar? – Just *a little*, please.

Few and *little* are often used in a negative sense to suggest disappointment or pessimism, while *a few* and *a little* are used in a positive sense to suggest that things are better than they might have been.

Numbers

There are two common kinds of number:

Cardinal numbers are used in all forms of counting that involve a total.

> **one** chair   **two** chairs
> **a hundred** people   **ten thousand** dollars

Ordinal numbers are used to talk about where something is placed in an ordered sequence. They are often used right after the definite article or after a possessive.

> **The first** horse to finish was disqualified.
> He's celebrating **his fifty-first** birthday in August.
> The company has just celebrated **its one hundred and fiftieth** anniversary.

Ordinals are mostly formed by adding **-th** to a cardinal number.

> fourth   twentieth   hundredth
> fifth   forty-ninth   millionth
> sixth   eighty-sixth   thousandth
> nine hundred and ninety-ninth

Some examples of exceptions are the words first, second, and third, and combinations which contain them, such as twenty-first.

Cardinal numbers can be used at the beginning of a noun phrase, like determiners.

> **one** chair   **two** chairs
> **a hundred** people   **ten thousand** dollars

or on their own, like pronouns.

> And then there were **three**.
> **Four** of them came toward us.
> The other **two** went to get help.

- Grammatically speaking, the words *next*, *last*, and *another* can also be regarded as ordinal numbers.

> It rained on the **last** day of our vacation.
> The **next** horse to finish was declared the winner.
> Oh no, not **another** birthday!

Ordinal numbers and the words **next** and **last** are sometimes called **postdeterminers**, since they come after the word *the* or a possessive.

> The **next** three days are going to be very exciting.
> The **last** three years have been difficult for everyone.
> We have to get off the bus at the **next** stop.

- An ordinal, as well as *next*, *last*, and *another*, can be used together with a cardinal number in the same noun phrase.

> The **first three** correct entries will win a prize.
> He scored **another two** goals before the end of the match.

- To show that a cardinal number is only approximate, the word some is often used before it.

> **Some two hundred** people gathered in the pouring rain.

Distributives

Distributives are determiners that are used to talk about how something is shared out or divided.

The distributives are *each*, *every*, *either*, and *neither*. They are used with a singular countable noun.

> *Each child* was given a balloon.
> I remember *every detail* of our conversation.
> *Either child* could win the prize.
> *Neither plan* was successful.

– *Each* and *every* are not used with proper nouns.

– *Each* is used to refer to separate persons or things in a group of two or more.

> Four girls came and *each one* sang a song.
> *Each ticket* should have a number on the back.

– *Every* is used to refer to all the persons or things in a group of three or more.

> *Every teacher* has a key to the building.
> Katrina danced with *every boy* at the party.

– *Every* can be used in front of ordinal numbers. "*Every second house*" means *the second house, the fourth house, the sixth house*, and so on.

> I have to work *every third weekend*.
> *Every fourth block* has a fire hydrant.

– *Either* is used to talk about one of two people or things.

> *They did not appoint **either** man as captain.*
> ***Either** restaurant would suit me.*

– *Neither* is used to exclude both of two people or things that are being referred to.

> *They appointed **neither** man as captain.*
> ***Neither** restaurant is cheap enough.*

Exclamatives

Exclamatives are used to introduce an exclamation of surprise, admiration, or a similar emotion.

The exclamatives are: *what*, *such*.

Exclamations introduced by one of these words consist either of:

– the exclamative in a noun phrase alone (usually with *What...*).

> *What a laugh!*
> *What awful weather!*
> *Such good manners!*

– the exclamative and its noun phrase in a complete clause.

> *He is such a nice man!*
> *You always wear such beautiful things!*
> *What a pleasant surprise this is!*

Noun phrases with several determiners

Most noun phrases contain only one determiner or none at all, but if there are more, they follow a definite order. Determiners can be divided into four groups, depending on what other determiners they can be used with and the order that they follow.

There are two large groups:

A *the, this, these, that, those, a(n)*, and the possessives *my, your, her, his*, etc.

> *a* ripe orange   *my* young sister
> *this* ripe orange   *our* young sister

B *another, some, any, no, either, neither, each, enough, a few, a little*.

> *each* ripe orange   *another* sister
> *some* ripe oranges   *enough* money

The words in groups A and B are known as the **central determiners**. A noun phrase will normally contain only one central determiner.

- The group A and group B words cannot be used together, with this exception: words in group B may be followed by a group A word if *of* is placed between them.

> *some* of *those* oranges   *neither* of *my* sisters

There are two smaller groups.

C The smallest group consists of these words: *all*, *both*, *half*, *double*, and *twice*. These can be used on their own before a noun or before the group A determiners above. Some speakers of English prefer to insert *of* between *all*, *both*, or *half* and a central determiner.

> *All of the* visitors left the ship.
> *Half of the* oranges were thrown away.

- The words in group C are sometimes called **predeterminers**. The exclamatives *such* and *what* belong to this group. See p. 180 for more details about these.

D The words in the fourth group are, *every*, *many*, *several*, *few*, *little*, *much*, *more*, *most*, *less*, the ordinal numbers *first*, *second*, *third*, etc., and *last*. These can be used on their own before a noun,

> *Every* move was carefully recorded.
> She did **many** kind things.
> She has *few* friends.
> *Last* call for Philadelphia. All aboard!

or after the A group of determiners.

> *Your every* move is being watched.
> *The many* kind things she did went unnoticed.
> *Her few* possessions had been stolen.
> *The first* thing she did was call her mother.
> I will always remember *these last few* days.

- Words in group A can be used in combination with determiners in groups C and D.

> *Both* girls were reading.
> *Both my* young sisters are really naughty.
> *All* visitors must now leave the ship.
> *All the* visitors left the ship.

Adjectives

Adjectives are used with nouns to make the meaning more specific.
If you use the noun "*dog*" it can mean any animal of that species.
As soon as you say "*a large, brown dog*" you have given two of its
attributes (color and size). A noun is said to be **modified** by its adjectives.

Adjectives have two main features:

– most adjectives can go before a noun; this is known as their
attributive use.

> *a **tall** girl*
> ***green** grass*
> *four **badly behaved little** boys*

– most adjectives can also go after a link verb such as *be* or *seem*;
this is known as their **predicative**, or **predicate**, use.

> *The roses are **yellow**.*
> *The girls are getting **tall**.*
> *These books seem really **interesting**.*

Any word that can go into both of these positions is a normal adjective.
When used predicatively (after a link verb), an adjective can either
describe the **subject** of a sentence,

> *The roses are **yellow**.*
> *The girls are getting **tall**.*
> *These books are really **interesting**.*

or the **object** of the sentence. See also p. 11.

> *Anna painted the room **green**.*
> *The children drove him **crazy**.*

Adjective order

The order is normally:

– adjectives that describe feelings or qualities.

> **pleasant** childhood memories
> **beautiful** brown hands

– adjectives of size, age, temperature, or measurement.

> some **hot** biscuits
> a **rectangular** baking dish
> those **nice young** girls
> a **big** smile

– adjectives of color.

> the **green** hills of home
> stylish **brown** shoes
> her beautiful **blue** eyes

– adjectives of nationality or origin.

> those friendly **Spanish** girls
> both the small gray **Irish** horses
> an elegant **French** woman

– adjectives denoting the substance or material that something is made from.

> a large **wooden** door
> an elegant **silver** teapot

It is possible to use adjectives next to each other in English, but in practice more than four is uncommon.

> *a happy young blonde German* girl
> *beautiful old colonial brick* houses

- Adjectives before a noun are not usually separated by *and*, unless they are adjectives of color.

  > *a green and white* striped shirt
  > *a red and blue* flag

- Adjectives can themselves be premodified by adverbs of degree. See also p. 186.

  > *an* **extremely** *intelligent* student
  > *a* **very** *tall* man
  > *a* **fairly** *messy* apartment

Some adjectives can only be used predicatively (i.e., after a link verb such as *be*). Many of the members of this group begin with *a-*:

> *abroad, afloat, afraid, alike, alive, alone, ashamed, asleep, awake.*

> *Our balloon was* **aloft** *at last.*
> *Charles is* **ashamed** *of what he did.*
> *The child is* **afraid***.*
> *The girls were* **asleep** *and were not* **aware** *of the noise.*

When an adjective is used predicatively it may have to be followed by a particular preposition if the phrase continues.

She was glad.	*She was* **glad to** *help.*
He was afraid.	*He was* **afraid for** *his life.*
I was free.	*I was* **free from** *guilt.*
It is **devoid of** *interest.*	*He was* **intent on** *revenge.*

There are some adjectives such as *devoid (of)*, *intent (on)* that always have to have a following phrase.

Although attributive adjectives usually come before the noun that they modify, there are some that can go immediately after the noun, particularly when they are used with plural nouns, e.g., *absent*, *present*, *involved*, *concerned*. When these adjectives are used in this position they may have a different meaning from the one that they have when they come before the noun.

> *Everyone present was offered juice.*
> *The present government took over four years ago.*
> *The people absent from work were all ill.*
> *Let us toast absent friends.*
> *The dealers concerned were sent to jail.*
> *There were letters from concerned parents.*
> *I prefer to have a proper introduction before we speak.*
> *Do you live in the city proper or a near suburb?*

- There are some set phrases that always have an adjective immediately after the noun. These are essentially noun phrases consisting of noun + adjective.

> *the Surgeon General*   *a lion rampant*
> *the president elect*   *the Attorney General*
> *a court martial*   *the Prince Regent*

Premodifiers and postmodifiers

Adjectives, determiners, and other nouns can all be used to describe a noun more specifically; that is, they can be used as **modifiers**. Nouns can also be modified by prepositional groups (groups of words that begin with a preposition) and relative clauses added after the noun. See p. 269 for more about relative clauses.

To make it simpler to talk about any modifying word that comes in front of a noun, we can use the term **premodifier**.

> *a young* man   *these* onions
> *my aunt's* house   *the elephant* house

Those modifiers that come after the noun are called **postmodifiers**.

> *the young man* **with the guitar**
> *the person* **who met me**
> *the girl* **I was standing near**
> *the people* **involved**

Very few single-word adjectives in English are used only as **postmodifiers**.

> *riot police* **galore**
> *flirting* **101**

Comparison

The **comparative** form of an adjective is commonly used to compare two people, things, or states, when you want to say that one thing has a larger or smaller amount of a quality than another.

- If the second part of the comparison is mentioned it follows *than*.

    *Anna is **taller than** Mary but Mary is **older**.*
    *Emma is much **thinner than** when I last saw her.*
    *Online learning is **less expensive than** conventional college courses.*

- Comparison in which you are considering whether two people or things are equal is shown by using *as...as* in the affirmative and *not as...as* or *not so...as* in the negative.

    *Helen is **as tall as** Linda, but **not as strong**.*

The **superlative** form is used for more than two people, things, or states, when one thing has qualities that exceed all the others. Superlative adjectives have **the** in front of them, but it can be omitted in predicative positions.

    *That is **the smallest** camera I have ever seen.*
    *He gave **the least expensive** gift to his sister.*
    *I'll have whichever is **ripest**.*

There are two ways in which the comparative and superlative forms of adjectives are formed:

- You add *-er* (comparative) or *-est* (superlative) to the adjective. Adjectives with one syllable usually take these endings.

	comparative	superlative
bright	brighter	the brightest
long	longer	the longest
sharp	sharper	the sharpest

- If the word already ends in -e, then only -r or –st is added. If a word ends in -y, it usually takes -er or -est, and the -y changes to -i.

	comparative	superlative
wise	wiser	the wisest
pretty	prettier	the prettiest
weary	wearier	the weariest

- You add the word *more* or *most* in front of the adjective. Adjectives with three syllables or more use *more* or *most* in front of the adjective.

	comparative	superlative
fortunate	**more** fortunate	the **most** fortunate
relevant	**more** relevant	the **most** relevant

Adjectives formed from participles use *more* or *most* as well.

	comparative	superlative
provoking	**more** provoking	the **most** provoking
enthralled	**more** enthralled	the **most** enthralled

To indicate the opposite of both the -er/-est and the *more/most* forms of comparison, *less* or *least* are always used.

	comparative	superlative
sharp	less sharp	the least sharp
fortunate	less fortunate	the least fortunate
interesting	less interesting	the least interesting
involved	less involved	the least involved

> Adjectives with two syllables (including those that already end in -er) can follow either pattern or sometimes both patterns. If you are doubtful about a two-syllable adjective, use the *more/most* pattern.

	comparative	superlative
shallow	shallower	the shallowest
or	more shallow	the most shallow
polite	politer	the politest
or	more polite	the most polite

A small group of irregular adjectives have quite different forms for the comparative and superlative forms.

	comparative	superlative
good	better	the best
bad	worse	the worst
far	further	the furthest

Far also has the regular forms *farther* and *farthest* but they are less common and typically used only where the meaning is about physical distances.

Adverbs and adverbials

When you want to add information about *how*, *when*, *where*, or *to what extent* something has happened, you can use an **adverbial**. Many adverbials are members of the group of words called **adverbs**, but adverbials are not necessarily just single words. They can also be word groups, prepositional phrases, or even clauses.

Adverbials generally modify the meaning of a verb,

> I **really** admire your courage.
> They changed **hurriedly** into their pajamas.
> Monica hummed **softly** as she washed the car.
> The firecracker exploded **with a loud bang**.
> He ran **across the lawn** toward the house.

an adjective,

> Harry is **totally** mystified by the result.
> You must admit that he can be **pretty** boring.
> That is **completely** unacceptable.
> Fears like that are **very** real to the sufferer.

another adverb,

> I thought about it **quite** seriously.
> The children are behaving **remarkably** well.
> Ali objected **very** strongly to the plan.

a whole sentence,

> **Frankly**, I think he is lying.
> **Nevertheless**, we must give him a chance.
> **Honestly**, I didn't mean to be rude to you.

or a prepositional phrase.

We are really in a no-win situation.

Most adverbials are optional parts of a clause or phrase, but there are a few verbs that need an adverb to complete their meaning. See p. 81. Conditional sentences must also have an adverbial clause, usually one beginning with *if* or *unless*. See p. 266 for more about adverbial clauses.

Adverbials can be divided into:

– adverbials of **manner**, which express *how*: e.g., *slowly, with care, well*.

   *Two men were working their way **slowly** up the hillside.*

– adverbials of **place**, which express *where*: e.g., *there, here, up, in town*.

   *Two men were working their way **up the hillside**.*

– adverbials of **time**, which express *when*: e.g., *now, today, last night, lately*.

   *Two men were lost on the hills **yesterday**.*

– adverbials of **degree**, which express *to what extent*: e.g., *largely, extremely, much, by a hair*.

   *It was **largely** their own fault.*

– adverbials of **frequency**, which express *how often*: e.g., *rarely, often, sometimes, twice daily*.

   *Search parties went out **every hour**.*

Although adverbials change the meaning of clauses or phrases, they are usually optional parts of the group or clause.

> He coughed **nervously**.
> **Really**, I think you are mistaken.
> **In a fit of temper**, he slammed the door shut.

They stand outside the word, group, or clause that they are associated with. For example, the same adverb can in one sentence be part of the description of a verb, while in another sentence, it may modify the whole clause.

> I think she acted **honestly**.
> **Honestly**, who does she think she is?

The exceptions are that:

- some verbs must be followed by an adverbial to complete their meaning.

> Alice behaved **wonderfully**.
> Sylvia acted **unlawfully**.
> Justin sped **down the corridor**.

- some verbs require both an object and an adverbial to complete their meaning. See also p. 28.

> Ranjit put the folder **back**.
> Jamal stood the golf clubs **in the corner**.
> Clare placed the cover **over the crib**.

• New meanings can be made by combining an adverbial with a verb to make a phrasal verb. See also p. 80 for more about phrasal verbs.

> The car **pulled out**.
> Lydia **went away**.
> Things **are looking up**.

Adverbials are classified according to the way they modify a word, group or clause. In addition to the uses given on p. 191, one important use of a special group of adverbials is to show how a sentence relates to what comes before it. An adverb used in this way is called a **sentence adverb**.

> *Nevertheless, we must give him an answer.*
> *However, it's good advice.*
> *On the other hand, we cannot turn him down.*

Another use of adverbials is to let your listener or reader know your point of view about a situation. This is called a **viewpoint adverb**.

> *Foolishly, I gave him my address.*
> *Clearly, he deserves our help.*
> *Actually, I don't mind.*

A further group of adverbials, all of them adverbs of degree, can only be used with adjectives or other adverbs. Examples are *very, fairly, rather, quite, really, too, somewhat,* and *pretty,* which is informal. These are sometimes called **submodifiers** because they can weaken or strengthen the descriptive value of the adjective.

> *She seems **pretty** nice.*
> *Antwon is a **very** good tennis player.*
> *Kim gave me this **really** expensive bag.*

They are used mainly with adjectives of quality. An adverb can also be submodified by another adverb.

> *She began to cry, **very loudly**.*
> *Sometimes I think you're **too easily** impressed.*
> *It must have been done **extremely recently**.*
> *The car was **almost totally** submerged in the flood water.*

There are certain adverbs (and adverbials) that can only be used with verbs and so cannot modify adjectives.

- Most adverbs can be used:

– before the verb phrase or the subject

> *Happily, she ran over the sand dunes.*
> *Tearfully, he told his brother the whole story.*

– after the verb phrase or the object

> *She ran **happily** over the sand dunes.*
> *He was telling the whole story **tearfully** to his brother.*

– between the auxiliary and the main verb.

> *She was **happily** running about over the sand dunes.*
> *He was **tearfully** telling the whole story to his brother.*

- Some adverbs can only come **after** the verb, e.g., *back, up, down, sideways, clockwise.*

> *Suddenly the frightened animal ran **back**.*
> *They hammered the wedge in **sideways**.*

- A few adverbs can come **before** the main verb, e.g., *barely, hardly, little, rarely, scarcely, seldom.*

> ***Scarcely had she spoken** when it came crashing down.*
> *He **had hardly eaten** anything.*
> ***Seldom** have I seen such ridiculous behavior.*

Notice that a subordinate clause beginning with one of these words has the same word order as a question: finite verb before subject. These are called **broad negatives**, because they give a negative meaning to a clause.

Compare:

> They **never noticed** her presence.
> They **scarcely noticed** her presence.

> Some speakers take care not to place an adverb between the *to* and the **base form** of the verb in a "*to* **infinitive**." This is called a "split infinitive." There is no good reason to regard a split infinitive as an error; the choice is a matter of personal preference.
>
> > I need to **really** think hard about this.
> > I **really** need to think hard about this.

Adverbs with nouns and pronouns

While **adverbs** can modify most parts of speech, they normally do not modify **nouns** or **pronouns**. Much more common is the use of an adverb of degree to modify a whole **noun phrase**.

> Jason is **quite a skilled craftsman**.

There is a small group of adverbs that can modify nouns and indefinite pronouns.

> the **man downstairs**
> the **example above**
> **Almost everyone** brought a bottle to the party.
> Most of the **stores uptown** close at 6 p.m.

Form of adverbs

Most **adverbs** are formed by adding -*ly* to the end of the related adjective.

slow	slowly
clever	cleverly
annual	annually

Words that end in -*ble* drop off the -*e* before -*ly* is added. So do the words *true* and *due*.

sensible	sensibly
suitable	suitably
true	truly
due	duly

A common spelling mistake is to add -*ley*. This mistake is often made when the adjective ends in the letter -*e*. Note the correct spelling of adverbs formed from adjectives ending in -*e*.

extreme	extremely
divine	divinely
free	freely

Adjectives that end in -*y* change to -*i* before adding -*ly*, unless, like *sly* or *dry*, they have only one syllable.

happy	happily
greedy	greedily
sly	slyly

Some adverbs keep the same spelling as the adjective to which they are related. It is often difficult to tell at first whether the word is an adjective or an adverb. The general rule is to look at the other words that it occurs with. If it comes before a noun it is probably an adjective.

a short way   *a late meeting*
a long pause   *an early lecture*

If it relates to a verb or an adjective it is probably an adverb.

*The lesson **was cut short**.*
*We **met late** at night.*
*Don't **stay long**.*
*He **came in early**.*

Some adverbs have the same spelling as a preposition. They can be told apart if you look at the words they are found with. Prepositions are normally used in front of noun phrases, because prepositions must have an object.

*He rushed **in an attempt** to catch his bus.*
*She hurried **over her meal** because she was late.*

When the word is found without an object, especially at the end of a clause, it will usually be an adverb.

*He rushed **in**.*
*She hurried **over**.*

Just like certain adjectives, some adverbs have comparative and superlative forms and can be used with submodifiers.

*Kim treated Sharon **well**, Karen **less well** and Janice **the least well**.*
*Malcolm walked **the most slowly** of all of them.*
*Tariq acted **very kindly** toward him.*
*You must behave **much more sensibly** in the future.*
*This graph shows that girls performed **the best** at math this year.*

Superlative forms of adverbs are rare.

Pronouns

A **pronoun** is a word that is used in the place of a noun or a whole noun phrase.

Pronouns are commonly used:

– in place of a noun or a noun phrase that has already been mentioned.

> *Sam has to go to the airport. Can you give **him** a ride?*
> *The vice president and his wife came out onto the balcony.*
> *   **They** waved to the crowd.*
> *The mechanic tested the starter . **It** would not work.*
> *   **He** tried **it** again.*

– when we know who or what is referred to. When, for example, *I* use the pronoun I it is because it would be unusual to refer to myself by name.

> *I'm sorry I'm late.*
> *We'd better call and say **we**'re not coming.*

– when the name of someone or something is not known.

> *He's the man who came to the house yesterday!*
> *Who's she?*

Types of pronoun

There are seven different types of pronoun, classified according to their meaning and use.

The **personal** pronouns can be used as subject or object in a clause.

> *He gave her a box of chocolates.*
> *We saw them both on Friday.*
> *I can see you!*

The **reflexive** pronouns are used in object position in sentences where the subject and the object refer to the same person or thing. You must use them with certain verbs.

> *The puppy entangled itself in the leash.*
> *I've just cut myself on a piece of glass.*

Reflexive pronouns are also used for emphasis.

> *Never mind. I'll do it myself.*
> *The professor himself did not know the answer.*

The **possessive** pronouns indicate ownership.

> *Give it back, it's mine.*
> *Perhaps it really is theirs after all.*

The **demonstrative** pronouns indicate items that are near to or far from us.

> *This is Betty's and that is Pedro's.*
> *These are nice. Where did you find them?*

The **relative** pronouns are used to link a modifying clause to a noun phrase or to a clause.

> *I don't know what you mean.*
> *That's the girl who always comes in first.*

The **interrogative** pronouns are used to ask a question about the noun phrase they stand in for.

> *What would you like for lunch?*
> *Which should I open first?*
> *Who was responsible?*

The **indefinite** pronouns are used for a broad range of reference when it is not necessary or not possible to use a personal pronoun.

> *Everyone had a compass and a whistle.*
> *Neither wanted to give in and apologize.*
> *Much needs to be done.*

Personal pronouns

Personal pronouns are used as the subject, object, or complement in a clause. They are commonly found taking the place of a noun phrase when it is mentioned for a second time.

person	subject	singular object	subject	plural object
1st	I	me	we	us
2nd	you	you	you	you
3rd masculine	he	him	they	them
3rd feminine	she	her	they	them
3rd neutral	it	it	they	them

The 1st person pronouns refer to the speaker or writer. The 2nd person pronoun *you* refers to the listener or reader. In the case of *you*, there is only one pronoun to cover the singular and the plural, so that it is sometimes necessary to use a form of words that will make clear who is being addressed.

> *You should be ashamed.*
> *All of you should be ashamed.*
> *You must all stop writing now.*

In informal and dialectal English, people use other forms to distinguish singular *you* from plural *you*.

> *Y'all should be ashamed.*
> *You guys are late.*

When more than one personal pronoun is used with a verb, the order is normally: 3rd or 2nd person before 1st person; 2nd person before 3rd person.

> *She and I do not get along very well.*
> *You and he should share the cost.*

When two pronouns or a personal noun and a personal pronoun are the joint subject of a verb, the subject form of the pronouns must be used. Avoid the common mistake of saying, for example, *Jerry and me are...*

> *Jerry and I are going to paint the house ourselves.*
> *He and I are going to paint it.*
> *Melanie and I are going shopping.*

When either two pronouns or a noun plus a personal pronoun are the joint object of a verb, the object form of the pronoun must be used:

> *They decided to help Jane and me.*

The object form of a pronoun is used after a preposition. Avoid the common mistake of saying, for example, *between you and I.*

> *Between you and me, I don't like this place.*
> *Wasn't that silly of me?*

The object form is usual in everyday spoken usage. In formal and old-fashioned English, the subject form is used:

- after the verb *be*.

It's me.	(informal)
It is I.	(formal/old-fashioned)
I saw at once that it was her.	(informal)
I saw at once that it was she.	(formal/old-fashioned)

- after *than* in comparison with *be*.

John is smaller than him.	(informal)
John is smaller than he (is).	(formal/old-fashioned)
Sylvia is smarter than me.	(informal)
Sylvia is smarter than I (am).	(formal/old-fashioned)

Otherwise, *than* + **object** pronoun is necessary.

  She's probably done more than me.

- The object form is also used to supply short answers to questions.

  Who found Glen's watch? – Me. Aren't I clever!

Reflexive pronouns

Reflexive pronouns are used whenever a grammatical object refers to the same person or thing as the subject in a sentence.

person	singular	plural
1st	myself	ourselves
2nd	yourself	yourselves
3rd masculine	himself	themselves
3rd feminine	herself	themselves
3rd neuter	itself	themselves
General	oneself	

> I cut myself with the butcher knife. (direct object)
> John was surprised at himself. (prepositional object)
> John taught himself Latin. (indirect object)

The reflexive form *oneself* can be used to refer to a person in general, though many speakers consider this formal and use *yourself* instead.

> The first golden rule is not to take **oneself** too seriously. (formal)
> The first golden rule is not to take **yourself** too seriously. (standard)

Oneself can also be used as a substitute for the 1st person singular. If it is used like this, the subject pronoun should be **one**. Most speakers also consider this formal and use the second person instead.

> One asks **oneself** whether it is worth the trouble. (formal)
> You ask **yourself** whether it is worth the trouble. (standard)

Some verbs take a reflexive pronoun only in particular uses of the verb.

> Jeremy introduced **himself**.
> The cat washed **itself**.

The reflexive pronoun can be left out if it is obvious that the subject was performing the action of the verb on him- or herself.

> Jeremy **washed** and **dressed**, then went out.

When a preposition is followed by a pronoun, the pronoun is normally in the object form.

> They all looked at **him** in silence.

If that pronoun refers to the subject of the main verb, however, it must be a reflexive pronoun.

> She looked at **herself** in the mirror.

- The reflexive can be used to make something you say stronger. To make a strong point, we sometimes use a normal subject or object pronoun and a reflexive pronoun as well.

> He told me **himself** that he was leaving.
> I'll do it **myself**.

- The reflexive can also be used with or without *by* meaning "alone" or "without help."

> I think you should try and do it **yourself**.
> Did she do that all by **herself**?

The compound pronouns *each other* and *one another* are not true reflexives. They are used when two or more subjects take part in the same action that affects both of them. They are sometimes called **reciprocals**.

> They should stop blaming **one another**.
> We will always love **each other**.

Possessive pronouns

Possessive pronouns are used when you want to indicate who owns or is associated with an item.

> *All those books are **hers**.*
> *Those suitcases are **ours**.*
> *Are you selling those books? I'd never sell any **of mine**.*
> *Those awful cousins **of yours** are here.*
> *This TV is really cheap. – Yes, **ours** was a bit more expensive, but better quality.*

There are separate forms for the singular and the plural except in the 2nd person. In the 3rd person singular the form changes to match the gender of the possessor.

> *I'm looking for Helen's sneakers. Perhaps these are **hers**.*
> *These are our seats and the ones in front are **yours**.*

possessive determiner	possessive pronoun
my	*mine*
your (singular)	*yours*
his	*his*
her	*hers*
its	*(no form)*
our	*ours*
your (plural)	*yours*
their	*theirs*

Note that none of these words should be spelled with an apostrophe. Avoid the common mistake of writing *it's* for the possessive form. *It's* is a short form for *it is*.

The demonstrative pronouns

The demonstrative pronouns are used instead of a noun phrase to indicate distance in time or space in relation to the speaker. They also indicate grammatical number (singular or plural).

	singular	plural
near far	this that	these those

- The demonstrative pronouns are the same words as demonstrative determiners; how they are used determines which of these roles they fill. See also p. 160. Usually a demonstrative pronoun substitutes for a noun phrase that contains the same word being used as a determiner. In speech, demonstrative pronouns are often accompanied by a body movement that indicates the noun being talked about, or in a context where both listener and speaker know what object is being referred to and so need not name it.

> *Would you like to share some of this pizza with me?*
> *Would you like to share **this** with me?*
> *I'd like you to put these things away before we go.*
> *I'd like you to put **these** away before we go.*

- It is impolite to use a demonstrative pronoun to refer directly to a person, except when making introductions.

> *John, **this** is Harry Forbes, my colleague.*
> ***This** is my husband, Rob.*
> *Mom, **this** is my former teacher, Miss Evans.*

Relative pronouns

The relative pronouns are the words *who, whom, which,* and *that.*

	person	*thing*
subject	**who** or **that**	**which** or **that**
object	**whom** or **that**	**which** or **that**
possessive	**whose**	**whose**

The function of a relative pronoun is to link a subordinate clause to a main clause or to some other sentence element.

> **He might lose his job,** *which would be disastrous.*
> **Tim gave away all the money** *that was left.*

A subordinate clause introduced by a relative pronoun is called a **relative clause**.

Relative pronouns refer back to a noun phrase or pronoun that has just been mentioned. All relative pronouns must come as near as possible to the start of the clause that they are in. The only words that normally come before them in the clause are prepositions or conjunctions.

The choice of relative pronoun is influenced as follows:

– *that* is the most usual pronoun, but note that it never has a preposition before it. It can introduce both human and nonhuman subjects or objects.

> *This is* **the person** *that Annie was talking about.*
> *Here's* **the jacket** *that you forgot.*
> *This is* **the person** *about whom Annie was talking.*
> *That is* **a kind thought,** *for which I am most grateful.*

– *which* is not used for human subjects or objects. It can be used for nonhuman subjects even when there is no preposition involved, but *that* is more common.

> *That is* **the car** *which she has just bought.*
> *I have found* **a ring** *which you will love.*

– *who* and *whom* are restricted to human subjects or objects.

> *He introduced me to* **his friend**, *who had just returned from China.*
> *I liked* **the actor** *who was playing Oedipus.*

– in **defining** relative clauses (see p. 269), *that* can be used for all subjects. *Which* can be used for animals and inanimate things. For people you can also use *who* or *whom*.

> *I have found* **a ring** *that you will love.*
> *I have found* **a ring** *which you will love.*
> *She is* **the girl** *who was at Sam's party.*
> *She is* **the girl** *that was at Sam's party.*

The **object** form of the relative pronoun is used as the object of a verb or a preposition, but because *whom* is very formal, it is not often used: in everyday English, *who* is usually used instead.

> *The late* **principal** *of the school,* **whom** *we all remember with affection, died last week.*

> *I discovered* **who** *he was visiting.*   (standard)
> *I discovered* **whom** *he was visiting.*   (formal)

● In informal writing and speech, any preposition is placed after the verb phrase instead of before the relative pronoun.

> *The girl* **who** *Brian was talking* **to** *seemed nervous.*
> *The people* **that** *he had been working* **for** *that summer had offered him a permanent job.*

- A defining relative pronoun referring to the object of the clause may be left out entirely as long as the meaning is clear.

   *He is the **person** (that/who/whom) Annie was talking about.*
   *That is the **car** (that/which) she has just bought.*

Interrogative pronouns

The **interrogative pronouns** *who*, *whom*, and *whose* are used only for reference to people. The interrogative pronouns *which* and *what* are used for reference to things.

	subject	object	possessive
people	who	whom	whose
things	which what	which what	

Interrogative pronouns allow us to build a question around the thing that the pronoun refers to. See p. 236, where these pronouns are explained more generally under the heading of **WH-** words.

> **Who** is dancing with Dontay?
> **Which** of these books would you recommend?
> **What** do you do when you're on vacation?
> **Whose** are these clothes?

Who is used to ask questions about people in general.

> **Who** is that man over there?
> **Who** did this?
> **Who** controls the day-to-day running of the business?

What is used to ask questions about things in general. **What** can be either a subject or an object in a clause.

> **What** happened next?
> **What** did you have for lunch?

Which is used ask for identification of a particular person or a particular thing in a group.

> *Which do you prefer, working in theater or film?*
> *Which is your favorite Simpsons episode?*

Whose is the possessive form of the pronoun. It is used when a person is the possessor.

> *Whose is that sports car outside?*
> *Whose side are you on?*

- *Whom* is the object form of *who*. It is a formal word that most speakers avoid using in casual conversation, when *who* can be used instead. When writing, however, it is usual to use *whom*.

> Informal
> *Who do you have in mind?*
> *Who were you speaking to?*
>
> Formal
> *Whom do you have in mind?*
> *To whom were you speaking?*

- The object forms of the interrogative pronoun are used after a preposition. In informal and everyday usage, you can place the preposition at the end of the clause.

> *Who does this belong to?*   (standard)
> *To whom does this belong?*   (formal)

Indefinite pronouns

The indefinite pronouns are used when you do not know or do not need to say precisely who or what you are referring to. The noun phrase that they substitute for can refer to a person, a thing, or a group of people or things, in which gender and number are not made clear.

> **Someone** will have to tell her that she's failed.
> **Everybody** had a wonderful time.
> **Anything** is better than nothing.
> **Nothing** can make up for this loss.
> Some people like that sort of thing. **Others** don't.

The indefinite pronouns can be grouped according to meaning, as follows:

A General amounts and quantities: *most, some, none, any, all, both, half, several, enough, many, each.*

> **Many** find it impossible to cope.
> Congratulations from **all** at the club.
> Judging by the comments, **most** wanted her to stay on.
> Although we lost a lot of stuff in the fire, **some** was saved.
> **Enough** has been said on this topic to fill a book.

B Choice or alternatives: *either, neither.*

> Could you bring me one of those wrenches? **Either** will do.
> **Neither** was enthusiastic about a traditional wedding.

C Undefined singular or multiple persons and things:

someone	somebody	something
no one	nobody	nothing
anyone	anybody	anything
everyone	everybody	everything

> Note the form of *no one*: it is always spelled as two words.

- The pronouns in group C that refer to people can cause problems concerning the **number** and **gender** of a following determiner or pronoun. Traditionally, only the use of a following **singular** form was permitted after all of these words. Today, common practice uses the plural form *their* in order to avoid awkward expressions like *his* or *her*.

  Everybody has their ups and downs.
  Has anybody finished their lunch yet?
  No one in their right mind goes on vacation there in January.

Many of these pronouns, especially those in groups A and B, have the same form as determiners. See p. 160.

- The way to tell a pronoun from a determiner is to see if the word on its own is used as a subject, an object, or the complement of a verb; if it is, it is a **pronoun**. If, on the other hand, it is used in front of a noun, it is a **determiner**.

  As a pronoun:
  Both were given life sentences.
  Several managed to escape.
  I've found some!

  As a determiner:
  Both men were given life sentences.
  Several sheep managed to escape.
  I've found some scrap paper.

- The pronouns in Groups A and B are often used like partitives, with *of* and a noun phrase or a personal pronoun.

  None of the children was hurt, but most of them were really upset.
  Neither of his parents remarried.

Prepositions

A preposition is a word that relates different items in a sentence to each other. Prepositions are very common and most of them are short words. Most English prepositions have a number of different meanings.

Simple prepositions consist of one word, e.g., *in*, *on*, *under*. Complex prepositions consist of more than one word, e.g., *due to*, *together with*, *on top of*, *in spite of*, *out of*, *because of*.

Prepositions enable us to express:

– information about space and movement to or from a **place**.
– information about **time**.
– information about cause and purpose.
– information about means or instrument.

Prepositions are normally followed by:

– a noun phrase.

> *in* **time**   *over* **the edge**
> *under* **the table**   *together with* **my friends**

– an *-ing* clause.

> *Thanks* **for looking**.
> *He picked up some extra cash* **by working** *in a bar at night.*

– a relative pronoun (**WH-** word).

> *He's married to Rachel,* **with whom** *he has one daughter.*
> *The inscription uses characters* **with which** *I am unfamiliar.*

In everyday speech a preposition may end a relative clause rather than come before it. See also p. 270.

> *That's the girl we were talking **about**.*
> *That's the man (**who**) I gave the money **to**.*

A preposition needs an object–that is, a noun phrase that completes its meaning. A preposition and the noun phrase that goes with it is called a **prepositional phrase**.

A prepositional phrase can be used as an **adverbial**;

> *He put the flowers **on the table**.*
> *She shut the dog **in the kitchen**.*
> *He found the papers **in time for the meeting**.*

as a **postmodifier**;

> *The house **on the corner** has at last been sold.*
> *The flowers **on the table** are from Tim.*
> *A bird **with brilliant plumage** roamed the lawns.*

or as the **complement** of a verb or adjective.

> *Someone is **in the shed**.*
> *We were staring **at the accident**.*
> *I'm so sorry **for what I said**.*

- Prepositions combine with some verbs to make new meanings from the combination. These are one type of **phrasal verb**. See p. 80.

> *We **believe in** his innocence.*
> *I **stand for** justice.*
> *She **went through** a terrifying experience.*

The list below shows all the common simple prepositions. Some words can be either **prepositions** or **adverbs**, depending on how they are used and what they combine with. The words in *italics* are the prepositions that can also be used as **adverbs**.

> *aboard*, *about*, *above*, *across*, *after*, against, *along*, *alongside*, amid, among, *around*, as, at, atop, bar, *before*, *behind*, *below*, *beneath*, *beside*, *between*, *beyond*, by, despite, *down*, during, for, from, *in*, *inside*, into, like, minus, *near*, of, *off*, *on*, onto, *opposite*, *out*, *outside*, *over*, *past*, pending, per, plus, prior, pro, re, regarding, *round*, *since*, than, *through*, *throughout*, till, to, toward, *under*, *underneath*, unlike, until, unto, *up*, upon, via, with, *within*, *without*.

The example below shows adverbial uses.

> *He went* **in**.
> *I put it* **through**.

When a verb is followed by a preposition, there is often little or no choice as to which preposition to use, e.g., *rely* **on**, *speak* **to**, *give* **to**.

When there is a choice of preposition, the meaning changes with each:

> *check* **for**, *check* **on**, *check* **over**; *speak* **to**, *speak* **about**; *talk* **to**, *talk* **with**.

Prepositions allow us to express relationships. These are mostly to do with place and time. Some prepositions can be used with more than one meaning, depending on how we think about the time or place we are discussing.

Prepositions of location

Prepositions can indicate:

– the direction in which something is moving in relation to another person or thing: *toward, from, to, off*.

> They ran **toward** the police station.
> He took the road **from** the town **to** the state park.

– something or someone being enclosed: *within, in, inside, outside*.

> There is no wireless signal **within** the room.
> There seems to be something loose **inside** the control box.
> You have to stand **outside** the room while we make up some questions.
> Did you put the cheese back **in** the fridge?

– being at a certain point: *on, at, by, near*.

> Don't stand **on** the beds.
> I'll meet you **at** the library.
> There is a huge reservoir **near** where I live.

– movement over or onto a place: *over, across, on, onto*.

> Griffon jumped **onto** the back of the truck.
> He slid the package **across** the table.
> Tears flowed **over** his cheeks.

– location as a line: *along, over, on*.

> We walked **along** the bank of the river.
> Please sign **on** the dotted line.

Prepositions of time

Prepositions can also indicate:

– a point in time, a date, or a period of time : *at, on, in, during*.

> *The baby arrived **at** 9 p.m. **on** April 1st.*
> *They got married **in** June.*
> *I'll be with you **in** five minutes.*
> ***During** power outages we used wood for heat.*

– a period or point of time which marks a change: *before, after, since, until*.

> *We lived there **before** Mother died.*
> *I went to that school **until** I was sixteen.*
> *I usually go there **after** work.*

– the duration of some event (how long it lasts): *for*.

> *Helen stayed there **for** the whole of July.*

Prepositions of cause and purpose

Some prepositions indicate the reason something was done.

– cause or reason: *because of, for, from, through*.

> *The road was closed **because of** an avalanche.*
> *He did it **for** the money.*
> *They died **from** exposure to cold.*
> *She lost her way **through** carelessness.*

Prepositions of means or instrument

Some prepositions answer the question "how?" by telling us the way something was done or what was used.

– means or instrument: *with, by, without.*

> *We traveled* **by** *air to save time.*
> *He broke the door down* **with** *an ax.*
> *Can you find your way* **without** *a compass?*

Word order in sentences

The order of words in an English sentence is very important. A change in word order often results in a change of meaning.

Many other languages use **inflection**, a change in the form of words, to show how the parts of a sentence function. English has very few inflections, so the place that a word occupies in a sentence, its **syntax**, is the most important feature.

Neutral word order

Most sentences have a subject, and then something that is said about the subject, which is usually the rest of the sentence. This divides the sentence into the **subject** and the **predicate**.

> *John* (subject) *bought the tickets on Saturday* (predicate).
> *The wall* (subject) *was torn down* (predicate).
> *My elderly mother* (subject) *is completely deaf* (predicate).

Most English sentences put the information that they carry in this order, and so it is called neutral word order. When this neutral order is changed, the meaning of a sentence also changes.

> *The **cat** killed the dog.*
> *The **dog** killed the cat.*
> *The **child** watched the rabbit.*
> *The **rabbit** watched the child.*

Word order in simple sentences

Simple sentences are those that have only one clause. They are extremely common in all forms of written and spoken English. Simple sentences have a normal word order that varies according to whether the sentence is:

- a **statement**,

> *I saw you at the theater on Saturday night.*
> *I didn't see you at the theater on Saturday night.*

- a **question**,

> *Did I see you at the theater on Saturday night?*
> *Didn't I see you at the theater on Saturday night?*

- a **command**.

> *You **should buy** a ticket now.*
> *You **shouldn't buy** a ticket yet.*
> ***Buy** a ticket now.*
> ***Don't buy** a ticket now.*

Word order also varies according to whether the sentence is **negative** or **positive**.

Focusing

When we want to focus the attention of a reader or a listener on a particular word or phrase, we can use variations on neutral order, such as putting the subject last, splitting a clause into two, or repeating some part of the sentence.

Here are some variations of neutral word order that place emphasis on different elements of the sentence.

> *We used to call him "Fuzzy."*
> *"Fuzzy," we used to call him.*
> *Didn't we use to call him "Fuzzy"?*
> *"Fuzzy" was what we used to call him.*
> *It was "Fuzzy" we used to call him.*

Declarative, interrogative, and imperative statements

Each sentence in English provides some type of information. For example, a sentence can be a statement, a question, a request, a command, a denial or a response, etc. In English the choice and order of the parts of a sentence help us express these meanings.

Most statements and denials are in the **declarative**. An important feature of declarative sentences is that they have a subject that comes before the verb.

> *Our dog **eats** any old thing.*
> *Our dog **won't** just **eat** any old thing.*
> *The dog **has** already **been fed**.*
> *The dog **hasn't been fed** yet.*
> *We **have** already **won** several races.*
> *We **haven't won** any races yet.*

Most questions are in the **interrogative**. An important feature of interrogative sentences is that they normally have a subject that comes after an auxiliary verb.

> ***Does** your dog **eat** any old thing?*
> ***Has** the dog already **been fed**?*
> ***Hasn't** the dog **been fed** yet?*
> ***Have** you **won** any races yet?*
> ***Haven't** you **won** any races yet?*

If the subject does come first it will be a special question word.

> ***Who won** the race?*
> ***Which** team **was** it?*

- Exceptionally, we can ask questions using the declarative. We do this by using a special tone of voice.

You're telling me he has a new car? I don't believe it.
It's raining again? That makes three days in a row.

Many commands are in the **imperative**. Commands in the imperative have no word that acts as a subject, though the subject is understood to be you. Commands in the imperative can sometimes sound rude or impatient.

Eat up. We have to go!
Leave me alone.
On your marks, get set ... go!

- We can make a **request**, which is a type of command, sound more polite by using the interrogative.

Would you feed the dog, please?
Would you mind shutting the door?
Could I have that now? Thank you.

Not all imperative sentences are orders or commands. They can be social expressions whose purpose is to express a feeling or to convey information.

Have a nice day.
Get well soon.
Help yourselves to coffee.

There is also a **subjunctive** form. It may be used when you want to talk about an improbable or unlikely situation.

If I were governor, I'd spend more money on education.
I'd take the offer if I were you.

The declarative

The **declarative** is used to make statements. A statement is usually the expression of a fact or of an opinion. Statements can be both positive or negative.

> *Chana is working today after all.*
> *Conor wasn't reading your diary.*
> *Helen was talking about you.*
> *I'm not going on vacation this year.*

Declarative sentences always contain a subject and a following verb phrase.

The normal word order for declarative sentences:

subject + verb phrase

> *Chana is working.*
> *Conor was reading.*
> *Helen stared at me in surprise.*

subject + verb phrase + direct object

> *Ross is writing a letter.*
> *Pam borrowed three library books.*
> *Stephen ordered vegetarian lasagna.*

subject + verb phrase + adverbial

> *Dominic was eating very slowly.*
> *Lyndsey was studying in her room.*
> *Mikhail laughed nervously.*

subject + verb phrase + direct object + adverbial

> *Dominic was eating his lunch very slowly.*
> *Lyndsey had been reading a book in her room.*

Certain verbs must have following objects, e.g., *see, find, prefer, take.*

> *She saw **her friend**.*
> *He found **a camera**.*
> *They took **a resort brochure**.*

Other verbs need, or can have, both a **direct** and an **indirect** object, e.g., *give, buy, offer.*

> *Laura offered* **me** *another cookie.*
> *Scott's uncle bought* **him** *a new bike.*

The word order can be either:

subject + verb + indirect object + direct object

> *Sultan gave* **the dog** *a bone.*
> *Stuart bought* **Marie** *a birthday present.*

or, with the addition of a word that indicates the recipient:

subject + verb + direct object + *to/for* + indirect object.

> *Sultan gave a bone* to the dog.
> *Stuart bought a birthday present* for Marie.

Another group of verbs must be followed either by an object and an adverbial expression, or an adverbial expression on its own e.g., *put, place, stand*.

> *Richard placed* **the computer** on the table.
> *Diana put* **her jeans** in the drawer.
> *Michael stood* **in the middle of the field.**

A further type of declarative statement has the same basic order of subject and verb as the **subject** + **verb phrase** + **direct object** (example on p. 226), but with a **complement** replacing the direct object. See p. 229 for more about complements and p. 11 for more about objects.

> *Brad seems to have been* **really worried** *lately.*
> *This dessert is* **delicious.**

Complements

Some verbs such as *be, become, seem,* do not have an object but a **complement**.

The **subject complement** is a word or phrase that tells us more about the subject.

> Alan is *a nice person.*
> Rajiv is *a psychiatric nurse.*
> Alison seems *very well balanced.*
> Amber is *herself* again.
> That's *it!*
> This is *for you.*

The subject complement is linked to the subject by a verb, and the order is as follows:

subject + verb + subject complement

Subject complements may be either noun phrases, pronouns, adjectives, or even prepositional phrases.

- Most adjectives can be used after a group of verbs that includes: *appear, be, become, look, seem, smell, taste,* etc. An adjective that is used in this position is called a **predicative** adjective and it is functioning as a **complement**.

> The tickets seemed *expensive,* but the show was *excellent.*
> These little cakes are *delicious.*
> Soon afterward, Patrick became *ill.*
> Jackie appeared *friendly enough* when I first met her.

Less frequently we find an **object complement**. The object complement tells us more about the direct object. It relates directly to the object and is placed after it.

Verbs that can take an object complement with their direct object include *make*, *call*, and *appoint*. The word order is as follows:

subject + verb + direct object + object complement

> *Peter's phone call made Maureen* happy.
> *She called me* a fool.
> *They appointed him* Director.

Word order in negative statements

In negative statements, the basic word order for subject and object is the same as in positive statements.

> *John has gone to school.*
> *John has **not** gone to school.*

The difference is that negative statements must contain *not*, and must have as part of the verb phrase, either:

– a **primary auxiliary** verb,

> *She **had not** arrived in time for lunch.*
> *Caitlin **is not** working this evening.*
> *Brandon **was not** reading your diary.*

– one or other of the **modal auxiliary** verbs, or

> *I warn you, he **may not** want to come.*
> *Ailsa **could not** see the road clearly.*

– a form of *be* used as a main verb.

> *That **is not** my book.*

The word *not* is added immediately after the first one of these auxiliary verbs. The main verb follows.

The word order is, therefore:
   subject + **auxiliary** + *not* + **main verb**.

A negative sentence may contain a modal verb and one or more auxiliaries as well.

> I **may** *not* **have** *gone by the time you arrive.*
> *They* **could** *not* **have** *seen her – they were asleep in bed.*
> *They* **should** *not* **have been playing** *in the road.*

In this case the word order is:
subject + **modal** + *not* + **primary auxiliary** + **main verb**.

If the verb phrase does not already contain one of these verbs, then it is necessary to add the **supporting auxiliary** verb *do*.

The present simple and the past simple tenses of main verbs take the appropriate form of *do*, and then add *not* followed by the base form of the main verb.

> *He runs.*
> *He* **does not** *run.*
> *He ran.*
> *He* **did not** *run.*
> *Lynn* **does not** *work overtime now.*
> *The bus* **did not** *run on Sundays.*

The word order is, therefore:
subject + *do-* **auxiliary** + *not* + **main verb**

See p. 234 for more on the supporting auxiliary.

- The contracted form of *not*, which is *n't*, can be used after any auxiliary verb except *am*. This is the most common spoken form.

> *He* **doesn't** *run.*
> *He* **didn't** *run.*
> *Lynn* **doesn't** *work on Sundays.*

She **hasn't** been to work all week.
He **isn't** going to come after all.
Bill went swimming but Ann **didn't** want to.

The full form with **not** tends to be used more in writing.

---

can + not is usually written **cannot**.

  She **can't** come.
  She **cannot** come.

- Other words with a negative meaning, **never**, **barely**, **hardly**, **scarcely**, **rarely**, do not change the order of words in a statement.

  She **doesn't buy** Vogue.
  She **never buys** Vogue.
  He **barely** earns enough to live on.
  I **hardly** think that is going to put them off.

The interrogative

The interrogative is normal for many questions. It contains a verb phrase that is followed by a subject.

There are two main types of question: those that can be answered *yes* or *no*, and those that have to be answered with a specific piece of information or a sentence such as *I don't know*. Each type of question has its own special word order.

Yes/no questions

Questions that expect the answer *yes* or *no* are called **yes/no questions**, or sometimes **polar questions**.

The **interrogative** is used to form yes/no questions.

The normal sentence order for the interrogative is:
   modal/auxiliary verb + **subject** + **base form** of the **main verb**.

> *Were the dogs barking?*
> *Have you been dieting?*
> *Can Mahmoud come too?*
> *Must you go so soon?*
> *Would you like a chocolate?*

When a sentence does not contain a modal verb or an auxiliary verb, the question is formed by placing a form of the supporting auxiliary verb *do* before the subject and following it with the **base form** of the main verb.

> *Does he enjoy tennis?*
> *Do they play a lot?*
> *Did that surprise his mom?*

Yes/no questions also have a negative form. **Negative yes/no questions** are almost always contracted. The negative in its contracted form *n't* comes immediately before the subject.

> *Doesn't he like talking about his childhood?*
> *Can't Peter have one too?*
> *Don't you speak French?*
> *Wouldn't you like to know a bit more about this?*

If the full negative form *not* is used, it comes immediately after the subject. The full form is very formal.

> *Does he **not** like talking about his childhood?*
> *Do you **not** want to know what it was about?*
> *Can Peter **not** have one too?*

WH- questions

When you want to get a detailed answer, not just *yes* or *no*, you must use a **WH- question** (or "**nonpolar**" **question**), which allows for many possible answers. The words *who*, *whom*, *whose*, *what*, *which*, *when*, *where*, *why*, and *how* are used to form this sort of question. These words are referred to as **WH-** words. See pp. 236–239.

> **Yes/no:**
> *Did you phone the school? – Yes, I did.*
> *Was she all right in the end? – No/I don't know.*
> *Have you seen Alice yet? – Yes, I have.*

> **WH-:**
> *Who was that man? – He's my geography teacher.*
> *What did he say when you told him the news? – He was too*
>   *surprised to say anything.*
> *When did you see Alice? – Last Wednesday.*
> *Where is Peter going? – To work.*
> *When did they arrive? – Yesterday.*
> *Why have you stopped going running? – The doctor told me to.*

WH- words

The **WH-** words are also called **interrogatives**. They are used for **WH-** questions. They can be determiners, adverbs, or pronouns.

WH- determiners

When used as determiners, *what*, *which*, or *whose* can be used to ask questions:

– about nouns

> *What book are you reading?*
> *Which plane is he catching?*
> *Whose jacket is this?*

– or about the pronoun *one* or *ones*.

> *Which one would you like?*
> *Which ones did Rudy want?*

● The determiner *which* can be used in questions about selecting. It can also be used together with the preposition *of* for the same purpose.

> *Which color shall we use?*
> *Which book sells the most copies?*
> *Which of these colors shall we use?*
> *Of all your novels, **which of them** did you enjoy writing the most?*

● The determiner *whose* asks about possession with reference to a person as the possessor.

> *Whose mother did you say she was?*
> *Whose bag is this?*

WH- adverbs

The adverb **WH-** words, *when*, *where*, *how*, and *why*, always make the sentence follow the interrogative word order.

− *When* asks about time.

> *When will they arrive?*
> *When shall I see you again?*

− *Where* asks about place.

> *Where are you going?*
> *Where have you been?*
> *Where is your coat?*

− *How* asks about manner or means.

> *How did you get here?* – *We came by train.*
> *How does this thing work?*
> *How did you manage to open the trunk?*

− *Why* asks about reasons and purpose. Questions with *why* are usually answered with a clause containing *because* to express reason, or with the *to* infinitive to express purpose.

> *Why is the baby crying?* – *Because she's hungry.*
> *Why are you saving your money?* – *To buy a bike.*

− *How much* implies reference to a quantity; *how many* implies reference to an amount or a countable number of things but may leave out the noun referred to.

> *How much money did they take?* – *All of it.*
> *How much does it cost?* – *$4.20.*
> *How many packs do you want?* – *Twelve, please.*
> *How many do you want?* – *Twelve, please.*

– *How* can also be used with adjectives such as *old*, *big*, *far*, or with adverbs such as *often*, *soon*, *quickly* to ask about degree, rate, or timing.

> *How far is it to the airport? – About five miles.*
> *How often does he come? – Not very often.*

WH- pronouns

The **pronouns** *who*, *whose*, *which*, and *what* can be the subject or object of a verb.

> *Who can help me?*
> *Whose is the new sports car outside?*
> *Which was your best subject in school?*
> *What happened next?*
> *What have you got to take with you to camp?*

The interrogative pronoun *whose* is used when the question is asked about a person as the possessor of something. See also pp. 200–201 on interrogative and relative pronouns.

> *Whose is the motorbike parked outside?*
> *Whose is this?*

• The form *whom* is used as the object of a verb or of a preposition in very formal or old-fashioned English.

> *Whom did you talk to?*
> *Whom would you rather have as a boss?*

Modern English usage prefers *who* instead of *whom* in all but the most formal contexts.

> *Who did you talk to?*
> *Who would you rather have as a boss?*

When *whom* is used as the object of a preposition, it normally follows the preposition.

>*To whom did you speak?*
>*With whom did she go?*

When *who* is used, the preposition is placed at the end of the clause.

>*Who did you speak to?*
>*Who did she go with?*

The **WH-** subject pronouns are found in the same sentence order as statements:
WH- subject pronoun + the main verb.

>*Who can help me?*
>*Whose is that motorbike parked outside?*
>*Which was your best subject in school?*
>*What happened next?*

The **WH-** object pronouns make the sentence take the word order of a question:
WH- object pronoun + primary or modal auxiliary + subject + base form of the verb.

>**What** *do you have to take with you to camp?*
>**What** *has Jonathan done now?*

- The exception to this is in informal spoken English, when the speaker wants to show shock or disbelief.

>*You did **what**?*

Sentence tags

Tags are short additions that look like questions, used at the end of a declarative sentence. They are sometimes called **question tags**, but many sentences ending with a tag are not real questions. They are usually used to check that the listener agrees with what the speaker has said. Sentence tags are very commonly used in spoken English, but not in formal written English.

The tag is added to the end of a sentence. If the auxiliary verb *be* or *have* or a **modal** verb is part of the verb phrase in the sentence, then it is used as the verb in the sentence tag.

> It *isn't* raining again, *is it?*
> You*'ve seen* the program, *haven't you?*
> Well, we *can't jump* over it, *can we?*
> You *will come, won't you?*

If the main verb is in the present simple or past simple tense, the tag is made using *do*.

> He certainly *likes* eating, *doesn't he?*
> I *slipped up* there, *didn't I?*

In negative tags, *n't* is added to the auxiliary. Note that this contracted form is always used.

> He certainly *likes* eating, *doesn't he?*
> I *slipped up* there, *didn't I?*
> They *went* with you, *didn't they?*

- The more formal forms such as *does he not, did I not, have you not*, are sometimes heard in some regional varieties of English.

The pronoun in the sentence tag must match the subject of the main verb.

> **You** *aren't listening, are* **you**?
> **He** *reads a lot, doesn't* **he**?

Sentence tags can be **negative**

> *They* **went** *with you,* **didn't they**?

or **positive**.

> *Your father* **doesn't belong to the** VFW, **does he**?

Normally, when the first part of the sentence is positive, the tag verb will be negative, and vice versa. Sentences in which both parts are positive are less common. These sentences must be used carefully as, with certain tones of voice, they can sound aggressive or judgmental.

> *So you* **think** *I'm a fool,* **do** *you?*
> *Oh! You* **smoke** *now,* **do** *you?*

- The same sentence tag may have different meanings depending on the tone of voice that is used with it.

> Falling tone: statement
> *She's gone out, hasn't she.*

> Rising tone: question
> *She's gone out, hasn't she?*

The sentence can be a statement of fact or a question, depending on whether your voice rises or falls at the end.

Sentence tags are used in the following combinations:

- To say something that the speaker expects the listener will agree with. This doesn't always sound like a question:

positive main verb + negative tag

> Mary **will pass** her driving test this time, **won't she**?
> Richard **seems** to have lost interest in everything, **doesn't he**?

or **negative main verb + positive tag**

> Jessica **didn't care**, **did she**?
> Kerry **hadn't done** enough preparation, **had she**?

- To point out or remark on something, often something that the listener cannot deny. This frequently sounds more like a question:

positive main verb + negative tag

> You've just **bought** a new car, **haven't you**?
> Henry **has been** away already this year, **hasn't he**?

or **negative main verb + positive tag**

> Dexter **hasn't been** to see you, **has he**?
> Paula **wasn't** in your class in school, **was she**?

- To show interest in something. This often repeats part of what the previous speaker has said:

positive main verb + positive tag

> You **saw** him in town, **did you**?
> So, you **come** from New Mexico, **do you**?
> So you've just **come back** from skiing, **have you**?

When a tag is used to show interest in something, the sentence is often begun with *So*. This type of tag can also be used in a challenging manner.

*Oh, so you've been here all along, **have you**?*

After a command, a tag made with *will* or *would* makes an order more polite.

*Make me a cup of tea, **will you**?*
*Just wait a minute, **would you**?*

The imperative

Commands and orders

The **imperative** is used to give commands and orders. The form of the verb used for the imperative is the **base form** of the main verb, which is used without a subject.

> *Walk to the corner, turn right, and cross the road.*
> *Open your mouth and say "Aaaah."*

- Although the main feature of sentences in the imperative is that they have no **grammatical** subject, they do have an **understood** subject, "*you*."

The basic form of the imperative remains the same whether it is addressed to one or more people.

> *Come on, Mary; I'm waiting.*
> *Come on, girls; you're late.*

There is also a special type of imperative, using *let's*, that is used when you need to include the speaker. See p. 246.

The word order of a sentence in the imperative is:

verb + **object** (if needed).

The negative imperative is made with *do* + *not* or *don't*.

> *Don't lose that key.*
> *Do not come back without it!*

The uses of the imperative are as follows:

- to give an order.

> *Go away.*
> *Stop that.*
> *Keep quiet.*

- to give instructions.

> **Don't use** this spray near an open flame.
> **Apply** the glue thinly and **leave** it for ten minutes.

- to give advice or warnings.

> **Don't forget** to take your passport with you.
> **Be** careful!
> **Don't go** on the ice.

- to make an offer or an invitation.

> **Have** a piece of cake.
> **Come** over and **see** me some time.

The imperative of **do** + **a main verb** can be used:

- for polite emphasis.

> **Do take** your coat off.

- to be persuasive.

> **Do try** to eat a little of this; it will be good for you.

- Note that the imperative is not the only way to form a command or an order. You can also issue a command when you use a sentence in the declarative or the interrogative.

  I'm certainly not going to get it – you get it.
  Would you get it, then? I'm busy.

Making suggestions

Let's (*let* + *us*) + **main verb** is used in the 1st person plural only, especially when you are trying to encourage someone to do something with you.

It includes both the speaker and the hearer, so the subject that is understood is represented by the plural *we*.

  Let's visit Malcolm this weekend.
  Please let's go to the movies tonight.
  Let's pool our resources.

- Suggestions that start with *let's* often end with the sentence tag *shall we?*

  Let's call her now, shall we?
  Let's go for a walk after supper, shall we?

In ordinary English the negative is *let's not* + **main verb** or sometimes *don't let's* + **main verb**.

  Let's not worry about that now.
  Don't let's worry about that now.

In formal English, the negative is *let us not* + **main verb**.

  Let us not lose sight of our aims.

Do let's is the emphatic form.

> *It's a fantastic bargain; do let's buy it!*

- The uncontracted form *let us* + **main verb** is occasionally used in formal and written English.

> *Let us be clear about this.*
> *Let us hope that this will never happen again.*

The answer to a suggestion with *let's* is normally either, *yes, let's* or *no, let's not* or sometimes, *no, don't let's (...)*.

> *Let's call her now, shall we? – Yes, let's.*
> *Let's call her now, shall we? – No, let's not.*
> *Let's invite Malcolm over this weekend. – No, don't let's do that.*

The vocative

The imperative is often used with a **vocative**, in which you mention a person's name or some other way of identifying the person to whom a command or request is being addressed.

>*David, come here!*
>*Come here, David.*
>*Hey, **you**, stop talking!*

The vocative can be a proper noun, the pronoun *you*, or a noun phrase. The vocative can come before or after the main clause. A vocative forms a part of many questions.

>**Peter**, *do you know where I put the DVD?*
>*Have you seen Chris recently, **Jenny**?*

A vocative is also combined with an interrogative clause to form a request.

>**Tony**, *would you pass me the hammer?*
>*Could I speak to you privately for a minute, **Sunita**?*

When a vocative is used with an imperative clause, the sentence is usually a command.

>**Sam**, *get off there!*
>**You**, *come back!*

A command can also be phrased as a request.

>*Would you stop talking now, darling, and go to sleep.*
>*Would you get off there, please, Sam.*

A practical reason for using a vocative is to supply the missing but understood subject, so that the right person will understand the command or request, and act on it.

Note the punctuation: there should be a comma between the vocative part of the clause and the remainder.

As part of a command, except for urgent warnings, the use of the vocative is considered rude or abrupt.

The subjunctive

The **subjunctive** is used in English for situations that are improbable or that express a wish, proposal, or suggestion. It occurs typically after certain verbs. These include:

ask	*demand*	*insist*
order	*prefer*	*propose*
recommend	*request*	*require*
suggest	*urge*	*wish*

It is also used in certain set phrases and in formal forms of speech and writing.

> Lord **have** mercy!
> God **bless** you!
> God **help** us!
> Heaven **help** us!
> Heaven **forbid** that that should happen to me.
> **Suffice** it to say he escaped with only a warning.

The present subjunctive

The form in the present tense is exactly the same as the base form in all persons of the verb. That is, there is no -s on the 3rd person singular.

The subjunctive is used in subordinate clauses that follow verbs expressing a desire, a demand, a formal recommendation, or a resolve.

> I only ask that he **cease** behaving in this extraordinary manner.
> It is vital that they **be** stopped at once.
> Is it really necessary that she **work** all hours of the day?
> I demand that he **do** something to make up for this.

The clause containing the subjunctive is linked to the main clause with *that*.

- American English uses the subjunctive fairly often. The subjunctive is not common in British English. British speakers usually take advantage of other ways of expressing the same message, especially in less formal speech. These forms are also acceptable in American English.

> I only ask that **he should cease** behaving in this extraordinary manner.
> It is vital that they **are** stopped at once.
> It is vital **to stop** them at once.
> Is it really necessary **for her to work** all hours of the day?
> I demand that **he does** something to make up for this.

The past subjunctive

The past subjunctive form **were** is sometimes used with the 1st and 3rd person singular, in place of the normal past form **was**.

The past subjunctive may be used:

– after **if** or I wish, to express regret or longing

> If your father **were** alive he would help you.
> If I **were** rich I would buy a Ferrari.
> I wish I **were** taller.
> If only he **were** here now!

– after **as if/as though** and similar expressions, to express doubt or improbability.

> You talk to him as if he **were** your slave!
> Some people behave as though dogs **were** human.

Many people prefer to use the normal form of the past in this type of sentence. This is quite acceptable in ordinary spoken English but may be considered an error in writing.

*If your father **was** alive he would help you.*
*If I **was** rich I would buy a Ferrari.*
*I wish I **was** tall.*
*If only he **was** here now!*
*You talk to him as if he **was** your slave!*

Exclamations

Exclamations are short utterances that you make when you are very surprised or upset. They are not always whole sentences. Sometimes they are more like a noise than a word. In this case they are called **interjections**.

Ugh!   *Phew!*
Wow!   *Huh?*

Many exclamations consist of just one word.

Help!   *Nonsense!*
Dang!   *Hooey!*

Exclamations can also consist of:

– *what* or *such* + **noun phrase**

What *a pity!*
Such *long fingers!*
What *idiocy!*
Such *impertinence!*

– or *how* + **adjective**.

How *silly!*
How *kind of him!*

They may also have the form of a negative question.

Isn't *it a warm day!*
Aren't *they kind!*

- Another form of exclamation is when the hearer repeats part of the sentence that he or she has just heard. This is used when the hearer finds it hard to believe what has been said or is very surprised. This sort of exclamation is called an **echo**.

    *Richard's passed the exam. – **Richard's passed!** That's great!*
    *Salome's here. – **She's here!** What a relief!*

Responses

Responses are made in answer to a question or a statement by another person in conversation. Like exclamations, they may be full sentences, but can also be phrases or single words.

> *Yes.*
> *On Tuesday.*
> *I certainly will.*

Responses usually do not make sense on their own because their subject, predicate, or some other important piece of information is contained in what another person said.

Although a response may not have a subject or contain a main verb, it can be classed as a sentence, because a response uses our knowledge of what has just been said. The subject or the verb will usually be understood from the context.

> *Are you coming to the party tonight? –* **Yes**.
> *When are you going to Des Moines, then? –* **On Tuesday**.
> *Will you be doing some shopping? –* **I certainly will**.

- If the verb is in a simple tense you can use the supporting auxiliary *do* as the verb in the response.

> *Do you like zucchini? – Yes, I* **do**.

- You usually just use the first part of the verb phrase in a compound verb to make a response. That is, the first **auxiliary** verb or the **modal verb** becomes the response form.

> *Has Tamsin been here yet? – Yes, she* **has**.
> *Was Andrea crying? – Yes, she* **was**.
> *Can we leave early? – Yes, you* **can**.
> *Should I be doing this differently? – Yes, you* **should**.

Some speakers prefer to use the modal and the auxiliary form together.

> *Laurence would be running if it weren't for his injury.*
> *– Yes, he **would be**.*

Sentences and clauses

A clause is a group of words that contains a verb. The verb in a clause can be finite

> *Use* this pan for the pasta.
> He *missed* the turnoff.

or nonfinite.

> *To cook* pasta, always use a large pan.
> *Dreaming* about Jenny, he missed the turnoff.

Simple sentences

Simple sentences consist of one clause, in which the verb is finite.

> Ann *went* to the bank.
> She *withdrew* $100.

Two or more clauses can be joined to make a **compound** sentence or a **complex** sentence.

Complex sentences

Complex sentences are those that contain a **subordinate** clause as well as a **main** clause.

> When he arrives, *I'll call you*.
> *He stayed at home* because he felt ill.

A **subordinate** clause is one that contains information about the main clause. It will usually be introduced by a **linking word** such as *when*, *if*, *because*, or *that*. The linking words are called **subordinating conjunctions**.

Most subordinate clauses can come before, after, or within the main clause. Usually, when one clause is of principal importance and the other clause gives information about the principal one, we have a complex sentence with one **main clause** and one **subordinate clause**.

- The position of a subordinate clause – that is, whether before or after the main clause – is determined mainly by what you want to emphasize in the sentence.

    Since you seem to have made up your mind, I'll say no more.
    I stopped seeing her because she moved to Seattle.

Compound sentences

A compound sentence is one that consists of two **main clauses**, joined by a word such as *and*, *but*, or *or*, called a **coordinating conjunction**. Each clause is of equal importance and gives information of equal value. The order of the clauses can be very important for the meaning. For example, the timing of an action can be described by the order in which the clauses follow each other.

    He picked it up and ran over to her.
    He ran over to her and picked it up.
    I drove to Miami and went on to Key West.

Compound-complex sentences

These have more than one main clause and at least one subordinate clause.

    Angie came over and we decided to use my car because hers was acting up.
    He ran over to Julie, who was sitting at the end of the bench, and grabbed her handbag.

Joining clauses

Coordination

The process called **coordination** joins two short clauses of equal importance with a conjunction. Each clause becomes a **main** clause in the new sentence.

> *Ann went to the bank **and** withdrew $100.*
> *Dulcie goes to work **but** Courtney doesn't have a job.*
> *Brooke **(either)** stays at home **or** visits her family.*

The clauses are linked by words called **coordinating conjunctions**, such as *and*, *but*, *(either) or*, *neither*, *nor*, or *yet*. Conjunctions come at the beginning of a clause.

● If the subject of both clauses is the same, it does not have to be repeated in front of the second verb.

> *She came over **and** ~~she~~ gave me a hug.*

The conjunction *and* is used:

– to join clauses where there is no contrast or choice.

– to join more than two clauses; the earlier clauses can be joined by a comma, but the last two must be joined by *and*.

> *Ann got into the car, drove to the bank, withdrew $100,*
> *   **and** went shopping.*

The conjunction *but* is used to join clauses where there is a contrast.

> *She wanted to buy a new dress **but** she couldn't find one she liked.*

The conjunction **yet** is used, mainly in written English, to join clauses where there is a surprising contrast.

> He's a quiet man, **yet** he still manages to command attention.
> She was suffering from a knee injury **yet** she still won the match.

- The conjunctions *and*, *but*, *or*, *neither*, and *nor* are also used to join two phrases of the same kind,

> This book is useful for **planning and carrying out** research.
> **The former president and his wife** were there.

or two words of the same class.

> I use this chair when I am **reading and working**.
> Do you undertake **detailed or intricate** work?
> **Jack and Jill** went up the hill.
> This is a **complicated but intriguing** film.

In particular, *and* and *but* are used to coordinate pairs of adjectives in a predicative position.

When there is a positive choice between the subjects of two clauses, you use the pair of words **either** and **or** to join the clauses.

> **Either** you come to my place **or** I'll meet you at work. Which do you prefer?

If the subject of the joined clauses is the same, the subject is used in the first of the joined clauses only. This is often also true of any auxiliary verbs that may be present.

> Martin said he would **either** meet them for lunch **or** take them to dinner.

When it is used in this way *either* must come in one of these places:

– before the subject in the first clause of the group.

– in front of the main verb and after any auxiliary verb.

You can use *either...or* to join more than two clauses if you repeat the use of *or*.

> *Tripp said he would (**either**) meet them for lunch,*
>> *(**or**) take them to dinner, or have them over for coffee.*
> *Fayssoux can (**either**) come with us or take a taxi later.*

The use of *either...or* emphasizes that the two clauses are alternatives and cannot both be true. Compare *and/or*.

> *Tripp said he would meet them for lunch, **and/or** have them*
>> *over for coffee.*

The word *either* can be left out if the sentence meaning is clear. Some writers treat all but the final *or* as optional.

> *Shut up **or** I'll throttle you.*
> *Choose a menu option, use a keyboard shortcut **or** use the cursor keys.*

> You can use *or* on its own to join two or more clauses,
> but *either* cannot be used on its own.

When there is a negative choice between the subjects of two clauses, you can use the pair of words *neither* and *nor* to join the clauses.

> *It is **neither** possible **nor** desirable to invite them.*
> *Jane was **not** a fool; **neither/nor** was she prepared to be blamed*
>> *for the error.*

The word *neither* can be used on its own to connect two clauses if the first clause contains a word with broad negative meaning such as *not*, *barely*, *hardly* or *scarcely*. If there is a subject in the second clause, question order must be used.

> There was **barely** enough meat for the children; **neither did they** have any bread.
> Eric **hardly** saw the fight; **nor did he** remember much about the incident later.

- The words *either* and *neither* can also be used as a pronoun or as a determiner. Each can then be used on its own; it does not then have a joining function.

> **Either** book will do. It doesn't matter.
> **Neither** book is at all suitable, I'm sorry.
> You can have **either**.

- *Either*, or, *neither*, and *nor* can be used as conjunctions inside a noun phrase or a verb phrase.

> You can choose to study **either** Shakespeare **or** Keats.
> **Neither** Vimala **nor** Katie knew the answer.
> She is **either** desperate **or** just stupid.
> He didn't know whether **to stay or go**.

Subordination

When two or more clauses are joined by a conjunction other than *and*, *but*, *or*, or *yet*, one of the clauses is the main clause; the other clauses are **subordinate** clauses. The different types of subordinate clause include **noun** clauses,

> What matters most is **that you treat everyone fairly**.

adverbial clauses,

> They went outside **as soon as the rain stopped**.

relative clauses,

> This is the problem **that we're facing** at the moment.
> We stayed in Telluride, **which is in the Colorado Rockies**.

conditional clauses,

> Maureen plans to live in Belize **if she can get a job there**.

and **reported** clauses.

> She told me **that Philip was in Providence**.

Each of the subordinate clauses is associated with an introductory word that signals what type of clause it is that follows.

> **After** she had read the diary, she returned it to the drawer.
> **As** they were going downstairs, the phone rang.
> They aren't coming **because** they've had an argument.

These words are called **subordinating conjunctions**. They include:

– the **WH-** words

– words like *since, if, when, because*

– the word *that*, either on its own or used with another word
  e.g., *so that* or *supposing that*

– a phrase ending in *as*, e.g., *as soon as, as long as*

● Each of the subordinating clauses has a preferred position. For example, most adverbial clauses usually follow the main clause, although they can also come before the main clause.

> *Shall I do the shopping **when I finish work**?*
> ***When I finish work**, I could do the shopping for you.*

Reported clauses usually follow directly on from the main reporting clause. See p. 276.

Noun clauses

These are clauses that can be used as either the subject or the object of a sentence or in other places where a noun phrase is usually found. They are introduced by *that*

> *What I like about him is **that he always tries his best**.*

or by a **WH-** word, e.g., *who, when, where*.

> *I don't know **where you live**.*
> ***How the thief got in** is a mystery.*
> ***Why she acts like this** is beyond me.*

Word order after a **WH-** word is the same as in a statement.

> The subordinating conjunction *that* can often be omitted.
>
> I think *that he'll succeed*.
> I think *he'll succeed*.

Adverbial clauses

Adverbial clauses generally follow the main clause. The following are the main types of adverbial clause:

Time: sets the timing for the main clause.

> We should go *as soon as you are ready*.
> I'll call for you *whenever you like*.
> *Since she went away*, I haven't been able to sleep.
> *The moment he said it*, I started to feel better.

- may come before or after the main clause.

- introduced by *after, as, as soon as, before, once, since, till, the moment (that), until, whenever, when, while*.

Place: sets where the action of the main clause takes place.

> I put it *where nobody would find it*.
> He made an impact *everywhere that he went*.
> *Wherever you looked*, he was to be found.

- introduced by *where, wherever*, or *everywhere*.

Manner: sets out how the main clause was carried out.

- introduced by *as, as if, as though, how, just as, the way that*, or, informally, *like*.

> Mandy looked *as if she had seen a ghost*.
> Cameron wandered in, *the way that he does*.
> You have to fasten it *as though it was a shoelace*.
> The room was decorated *just as he had imagined*.
> Stop acting *like you own the place*.

Reason: sets out the thinking behind the action of the main clause.

> I don't want to go **because I don't like old movies**.
> **Since no one was ready**, I sat down and turned on the TV.

– may come before or after the main clause.

– introduced by *as*, *because*, or *since*.

Purpose: sets out what it was hoped would be achieved by carrying out the action of the main clause.

> Put it right there **so that it holds the door open**.
> Leave a bit for Becky **in case she's hungry when she gets in**.

– introduced by *so that*, *in order that*, *in case*, or *lest*.

• Purpose can also be indicated by *so as to*, *in order to* followed by the base form of a verb.

> I'm living with my parents **so as to save money**.
> He put the chair against the door **in order to hold it open**.

Result: sets out what happened when the main clause was carried out.

> Ben was **so angry that he kicked the wall hard**.
> Nina is **such a generous person that she's often short of money**.

– introduced by *so* + **adjective/adverb** + *that* or by *such a* + **noun phrase** + *that*.

Contrast: suggests that something else may need to be taken into account regarding the main clause.

> *However much you may want to spend your money, try to*
> *save a little each month.*
> *Although it had rained, the ground was still very dry.*
> *We must try to do something for the environment, even if we*
> *can't solve all the world's problems.*

– may come before or after the main clause.

– introduced by *although*, *even though*, *even if*, *however*, *much as*, or *while*.

Relative clauses

Relative clauses tell us more about nouns. They function somewhat like adjectives, and are found as **postmodifiers** in a noun phrase. The noun that is modified is called the **antecedent**. Relative clauses normally begin with *who*, *whom*, *whose*, or *that*.

These words are called **relative pronouns**. Note that some of them also function as interrogative pronouns. See also p. 209.

A relative pronoun can be the subject

> *The people **who live upstairs** are having a party.*
> *The dog **that bit me** had to be put down.*

or object

> *I don't like the music **that they are playing**.*
> *A man **whom I met on vacation** phoned last night.*

of the verb in the relative clause. If it is the object, the relative pronoun can be left out in ordinary informal speech and writing.

> *I don't like the music **they are playing**.*
> *A man **I met on vacation** phoned last night.*

Subject and object relative pronouns come at the beginning of the relative clause.

- A relative pronoun can also be the object of a preposition.

> *It was definitely Diana **to whom she was referring**.*
> *It's a great game **at which anyone can excel**.*

In informal English a relative clause can end in a preposition, especially if the relative pronoun is omitted.

> It was definitely Diana *that she was referring to*.
> It's great game *which anyone can excel at*.

Defining and nondefining relative clauses

There are two sorts of relative clause.

Some relative clauses act like an adjective by providing more information about a particular noun.

> The people *who live upstairs* are having a party.
> I don't like the music *that they're playing*.
> The girl *who was on the bus with us* is called Sonia.

These are called **defining** relative clauses or **restrictive** relative clauses. A defining relative clause is never separated from the noun by a comma.

The other type of relative clause adds extra information to the whole of the main clause. These are **nondefining relative clauses** or **nonrestrictive** relative clauses. This type of clause is separated from the main clause by commas. Note that this type of clause cannot begin with *that*.

> The man next door, *who works from home*, kept an eye on the house for us.
> Thomas went home early, *which was a relief to us all*.
> We stopped in Estes Park, *which is a good place for a picnic*.

Compare:

Defining.
My brother who lives in Canada is a lawyer.
(There are several brothers. The Canadian one is a lawyer.)

Nondefining.
My brother, who lives in Canada, is a lawyer.
(There is only one brother. He is a lawyer. He happens to
   live in Canada.)

Conditional clauses

Conditional sentences consist of a main clause and a **conditional clause** (sometimes called an *if-clause*). The conditional clause usually begins with *if* or *unless*. The conditional clause can come before or after the main clause.

> *We'll be late if we don't leave now.*
> *We'll be late unless we leave now.*
> *If we don't leave now, we'll be late.*
> *Unless we leave now, we'll be late.*

There are three main types of conditional sentence.

Type 1

The main clause uses *will*, *can*, *may*, or *might* + the **base form** of a main verb. The *if-clause* uses the present simple tense.

> *If you take the first bus, you'll get there on time.*
> *She'll be cold if she doesn't wear a coat.*
> *If you need more helpers, I can try and get some time off work.*

Type 1 sentences refer to the future. They suggest that the action in the main clause is quite likely to happen.

> *They will not finish their homework unless they start now.*
> *If you call early, you will get a seat.*

The use of the modal verb may or might in the main clause suggests that there is some doubt whether the main verb action will be achieved.

> *If you call early, you may get a seat.*
> *Mary might deliver your message, if you ask her.*

Type 2

The main clause uses *would*, *could*, or *might* + the **base form** of a main verb. The *if-clause* uses the past simple tense.

> If Jim **lent** us his car, we could go to the party.
> We would save $5 a day if we **didn't eat** any lunch.
> If burglars **broke** into my house, they wouldn't find any money.
> Would you be very angry if I **failed** my exam?

or the past subjunctive.

> If I **were you**, I'd phone her right away.

Type 2 sentences refer to an imaginary situation. They imply that the action in the *if-clause* will probably not happen.

> If I won the lottery, I would buy a cabin in Montana.
>   (...but I don't think I'll win the lottery.)
> If you didn't spend all your money on lottery tickets, you could
>   afford a vacation.
>   (...but you do spend all your money on lottery tickets.)

The past subjunctive is often used when giving advice to someone, especially about what the person should do.

> If I **were you**, I'd tell them the truth.

Type 3

The main clause uses *would*, *could*, or *might* + *have* + the **past participle** of a main verb. The *if*-**clause** uses the past perfect tense.

> We could have had a longer vacation, if we **hadn't spent** so much money on the house.
> If I **had known** about the exam, I would have paid more attention in class.

In Type 3 sentences the speaker is looking back from the present to a past time and event. The speaker is talking about what might have happened but did not, either because the wrong thing was done or because nothing was done. This type of sentence is used when making excuses, showing regret, blaming, or giving an explanation.

Type 3 sentences can usually be written without using *if*, by putting the auxiliary verb first in the *if*-**clause**:

> **Had I known** about the exam, I would have paid more attention in class.

Conditional clauses can also be used to talk about consequences, or to give an opinion about a situation in the following ways:

– The *if*-**clause** uses the present simple tense and the main clause uses the present simple tense. This is used to refer to universal truths.

> If you **heat** water to 100°C, it **boils**.
> Plants **die** if they **don't get** enough water.

– The *if*-**clause** uses the present simple tense and the main clause is in the imperative. This is used to give advice or orders for particular situations or sets of circumstances.

> If the alarm **goes off**, **make** your way outside to the parking lot.
> If a red light **comes on** here, **switch off** the machine.

- The *if-clause* uses the present continuous or present simple tense and the main clause uses a modal verb. This is used to make suggestions and give advice.

    > If you're **thinking of** buying a lawnmower, you **could** try mine first.
    > You **should** turn down the radio if you **don't want** the neighbors to complain.

- The *if-clause* uses *will/would* and the main clause uses a modal verb.

This is used to make a request or to give a polite order.

    > If **you'll** wait a minute, the doctor **can** see you.
    > If you **would** sign here, please, I'll be able to send you the books.

> Note that a *'d* in the main clause is the contracted form of *would*. However, a *'d* in an *if-clause* is the contracted form of *had*.
>
> > **I'd** have gone if **he'd** invited me.
> > I **would** have gone if **he had** invited me.
> > I **would've** gone if **he'd** invited me.

In the main clause the contracted forms of the modals used in speech and informal writing are:

| **I'd have** | or | **I would've** |
| **I could've** | | **I might've** |

Reporting speech

There are two ways of writing down or reporting what was said on any occasion. We can repeat the actual words used (**direct speech**),

> *Monica said, "**There's nothing we can do about it.**"*

or we can build the words into our own sentences (**reported speech**).

> *Monica said that there was nothing we could do about it.*

The words reported are normally accompanied by a **reporting verb**.

> *Monica **said/declared** that there was nothing we could do about it.*
> *"There is nothing we can do about it," Monica **replied**.*

Another name for reported speech is **indirect speech**.

Direct speech

Direct speech gives the actual words that the speaker used. It is common in fiction and other writing where the actual words of a speaker are quoted.

> *Monica said, "**There's nothing we can do about it**."*

The **reporting verb** may come before the words that were actually spoken, or after them, or at a natural pause inside the reported sentence.

> ***Monica said**, "There is nothing we can do about it."*
> *"There is nothing we can do about it," **Monica said**.*
> *"It's no good," **Monica said**, "we'll just have to ask for help."*

- The comma comes inside the quotation marks.

- Typical reporting verbs are: *agree, answer, ask, inquire, explain, reply, respond, say, tell,* and *wonder.*

The subject and the reporting verb are sometimes reversed.

> *"There is nothing we can do about it,"* **said Monica**.

The actual words spoken always begin with a capital letter, unless the reporting verb comes within a sentence. They are separated from the reporting verb by a comma, unless they are followed by a question mark or an exclamation.

> *"Why did you do it?" she asked.*
> *"Oh, mind your own business!" he snapped.*

- The words spoken are enclosed in double quotation marks.

> **"Have you been to the new shopping mall yet?"** *enquired Shona.*

> **"I've already seen it,"** *John replied.*

- Single quotation marks are used to set off a quotation within a quotation (see p. 298.)

Reported speech

Reported speech or **indirect speech** reports something that was said, but does not use the actual words that the speaker uttered.

>*Lynn asked whether Pryce had been to the new shopping mall.*
>*Pryce replied that she hadn't, but she had heard that there were some really cool shops there.*

Reported speech always has two clauses. The words that are spoken are put in a **reported clause**. There is also a **main clause** that contains a **reporting verb**. The main clause with the reporting verb usually comes before the **reported clause**.

>*Katie **told me** that Alison is going to resign.*
>*Peter **asked** whether Mandy was feeling better.*

The reporting verb in the main clause tells us how the sentence was uttered, e.g., *comment, remark, say, tell*. If the reported clause is a **statement**, the main clause is linked to the reported clause by *that*.

>*Mary said **that** her favorite actor was Matt Damon.*
>*John replied **that** he preferred Scarlett Johansson.*

If the reported clause asks a question, the main verb will be a question verb e.g., *ask, inquire, wonder, want to know*. The link between the main clause and the reported clause will be *if* or ***whether***.

• The linking word ***that*** can be left out after most reporting verbs,

>*Jamie told Dad **(that)** he had passed his driving test.*
>*Lawanda said Alan had been accepted at drama school.*

but the links *if* or ***whether*** cannot be left out.

>*Miriam asked **if** she could borrow Leonie's mp3 player.*
>*Evelyn wondered **whether** the concert would be sold out.*

- Speech in a reported clause is not separated from the reporting verb by a comma, is not enclosed in quotation marks, and does not begin with a capital letter unless it is a proper noun. Reported questions are not followed by question marks.

Some writers put the main clause after the reported clause. In this case, no link is required. This is somewhat informal.

> *Harry Potter was on that night,* **Mary said**.

Reported clauses can also be used to express what is in someone's mind as well as what is actually spoken.

> *Evelyn* **wondered whether** *the concert would be sold out*.
> *Charlotte* **thought that** *she had better go and see her family*.

Changes in the reported words

When you use reported speech, the words put into the reported clause do not exactly match the words actually spoken.

> "I'll leave here at 8:30 on Friday."
> She says **that she will leave there at 8:30 on Friday**.
> "I'm looking forward to seeing you."
> She says **she's looking forward to seeing us**.

Pronouns and **possessive determiners** have to change in reported speech because of the change of speaker, e.g., I may become *she*; *you* may become *us* or *him*.

"*I believe you.*"
She said that ***she*** *believed* ***us***.

"*I'm leaving you.*"
She said that ***she*** *was leaving* ***him***.

"*I've finished.*"
She said that ***she had finished***.

Expressions of place and time may also have to change. *Here* may become *there* or *home*; *Friday* may become *in three days' time*.

"*I've been here before.*"
She said that she ***had been there before***.

"*I'll see you on Monday.*"
She said that she would see him ***in three days' time***.

Tense in reported clauses

The verb may also change, e.g., *must* becomes *had to* in reported speech. The most common change is a change of tense.

"*Hello Jake? It's me, Shiloh. I've arrived here on time, and I'm going to take a bus to your place. There's one coming now, so I'd better run.*"

Shiloh called to say that ***she'd*** *arrived* ***there*** *on time and* ***was going to*** *take a bus to* ***our*** *place. Then she said that one* ***was*** *coming* ***at that very moment***, *so* ***she had to*** *run.*

A reporting verb in the present tense can be used in the main clause when you report on a letter or on a recent conversation, such as a telephone conversation.

"Hello, Jake? I've arrived here on time, and I'm going to take a
   bus to your place."
Shiloh has just phoned. She **says** that she has arrived on time
   and that **she's coming** here by bus.

However, it is more common to use a past tense when reporting speech.

The changes of tense may be summarized as follows:

direct speech	reported speech
present simple	past simple
present continuous	past continuous
present perfect	past perfect
present perfect continuous	past perfect continuous
past simple	past perfect or past simple
future	conditional

Questions

Verb tenses in reported questions undergo the same changes as in
statements. See p. 278.

"Are you ready?"
He asked (us) if/whether we **were** ready.

"What time is it?"
He asked what time it **was**.
"Where has Jim gone?"
He wanted to know where Jim **had gone**.

Reporting verbs for questions include *ask, inquire, want to
know*, and *wonder*.

Direct **yes/no** questions are linked to the reporting clause by *if* or *whether*. **WH-** question words, e.g., *who, when, where*, are used in both direct and indirect questions.

> *"Are you ready?"*
> *He asked (us) if/whether we* **were** *ready.*
> *"What time is it?"*
> *He asked what time it* **was**.
> *"Where has Jim gone?"*
> *He wanted to know where Jim* **had gone**.

- The word order in a reported question is the same as that of a direct statement. Question order is not used in reported speech: no part of the verb comes before the subject.

Orders and requests

Orders are reported with *tell* + **object** + *to* **infinitive**.

> *"Stop calling me names!"*
> *She* **told him to stop** *calling her names.*

Requests for action are reported with *ask* + **object** + *to* **infinitive**.

> *"Please don't leave your things on the floor."*
> *She asked us* **not to leave** *our things on the floor.*

Requests for objects are reported with *ask for* + **object**.

> *"Can I have the salt, please?"*
> *He* **asked for the salt**.

- The reporting verb can be used in the passive.

> *"Don't park here, it's reserved for the doctors."*
> *I was* **told not to park** *there.*

Suggestions, advice, promises, etc.

A variety of verbs can be used for reporting suggestions and similar types of speech. Some of these are:

– *suggest, insist on*   + present participle

> "Let's go to the zoo."
> **He suggested going to the zoo.**

– *advise, invite, warn*   + direct object + *not* + *to* infinitive

> "I wouldn't buy that one, if I were you."
> She advised me **not to buy** that one.

– *refuse, threaten*   + *to* infinitive

> "I'm not telling you!"
> She **refused to tell** me.

– *offer, promise*   + *to* infinitive

> "Don't worry; I'll help you."
> He **offered to help** me.

Punctuation

The apostrophe (')

Misusing or omitting the apostrophe is one of the commonest punctuation errors.

Showing possession

The apostrophe (') is used to show that something belongs to someone. It is usually added to the end of a word and followed by an -s.

- -'s is added to the end of singular words.

    a baby's stroller
    Hannah's book
    a child's cry

- -'s is added to the end of plural words not ending in -s.

    children's games
    women's clothes
    people's lives

- An apostrophe alone (') is added to plural words ending in -s.

    Your grandparents are your parents' parents.
    We're campaigning for workers' rights.
    They've hired a new ladies' fashion guru.

- -'s is added to the end of names and singular words ending in -s.

    James's car
    the octopus's tentacles

- If the word is a famous name an apostrophe only, without the *s*, is sometimes preferred.

  > *Dickens' novels*
  > *Sophocles' tragedies*

- -'s is added to the end of people or their names to indicate that you are talking about their home.

  > *I'm going over to Harry's for dinner tonight.*
  > *I stopped by Mom's this afternoon, but she wasn't in.*

-'s can also be added to:

- whole phrases

  > *My next-door neighbor's dog was barking away like mad.*
  > *John and Cath's house was on TV last night.*

- indefinite pronouns

  > *Is this anybody's pencil sharpener?*
  > *It's nobody's fault but mine.*

- each other

  > *We're getting used to each other's habits.*
  > *We kept forgetting each other's names.*

When the possessor is an inanimate object (rather than a living thing), the apostrophe is not used and the word order is changed.

> *the middle of the street* (not *the street's middle*)
> *the front of the house* (not *the house's front*)

To test whether an apostrophe is in the right place, think about who the owner is.

the boy's books (= the books belonging to the boy)
the boys' books (= the books belonging to the boys)

Note that:

– An apostrophe is *not* used to form possessive pronouns such as *its*, *yours*, or *theirs*.

– An apostrophe is *not* used to form the plurals of words such as *potatoes* or *tomatoes*.

With letters and numbers

An apostrophe is used in front of two figures referring to a year or decade.

College students rioted in '68 (short for "1968").
He worked as a schoolteacher during the '80s and early '90s.

An apostrophe can be used in plurals of letters and numbers to make them more readable. It is sometimes used to show the plural of words and abbreviations spelled in all capital letters.

Mind your p's and q's.
His 2's look a bit like 7's.
She got straight A's in her exams.
He developed a scam to rob ATM's.

REMEMBER

it's = it is, e.g., *It's a holiday today.*
its   = belonging to it, e.g., *The dog was scratching its ear.*

Contracted forms

An apostrophe is used in shortened forms of words to show that one or more letters have been left out. Contractions are usually shortened forms of auxiliary verbs.

be
I'm
We/you/they're (are)
He/she/it/one's (is)
(had)

have
I/we/they've (have)
He/she/it/one's (has)
I/we/you/he/she/it/one/they'd

would
I/we/you/he/she/it/they'd (would)

or the negative *not*.

not
We/you/they aren't
He/she/it/one isn't
I/we/they haven't
He/she/it/one hasn't

In order to work out what the contracted forms *'s* and *'d* represent, you need to look at what follows them:

– If *'s* is followed by an *-ing* form, it represents the auxiliary *is*.

She's **reading** a book about the ancient Egyptians.
He's **going** to Cancun for his vacation.

– If *'s* is followed by an adjective or a noun phrase, it represents the main verb *is*.

She's **nervous** about meeting my parents.
He's **brilliant** at math.

– If *'s* is followed by a past participle, it can represent *is* as it is used in the passive,

> He's **portrayed** by the media as a kindly old grandfather.
> It's often **said** that rock stars are frustrated actors.

or *has* as it is used in the present perfect.

> She's **broken** her wrist.
> It's **been** ages since we last saw you.

– If *'s* is followed by *got* or *gotten*, it represents the auxiliary *has*.

> She's **got** two brothers and one sister.
> It's **gotten** colder in the last few days.

– If *'d* is followed by a past participle, it represents the auxiliary *had*.

> I'd **raced** against him before, but never in a marathon.
> She couldn't believe what she'd **done**.

– If *'d* is followed by a base form, it represents the modal auxiliary *would*.

> I'd **give** up now, if I were you.
> When we were kids we'd **spend** hours out on our bikes.

– If *'d* is followed by *rather* or *better*, it represents the modal auxiliary *would*.

> We'd **better** go home soon.
> I'd **rather** not talk about that.

The comma (,)

The comma marks a short pause between elements in a sentence.

Separating main clauses

Main clauses that are joined together with *and* or *but* do not normally have a comma before the conjunction unless the two clauses have different subjects.

> *You go out of the door and turn immediately left.*
> *It was cold outside, but we decided to go out for a walk*
>   *anyway.*

Separating subordinate clauses from main clauses

Commas are normally used if the subordinate clause comes before the main clause.

> *If you have any problems, just call me.*
> *Just call me if you have any problems.*

Sometimes a comma is used even when the main clause comes first, if the clauses are particularly long.

> *We should be able to finish the work by the end of the week,*
>   *if nothing unexpected turns up between now and then.*

Separating relative clauses from main clauses

Commas are used to mark off nondefining relative clauses (see p. 270). This is the type of clause that adds to information about a noun or noun phrase.

> My next-door neighbor, who works from home, is keeping
>   an eye on the house while we're away.
> She moved to Los Angeles, where she was immediately
>   successful as a singer–songwriter.

Commas are not required in defining relative clauses (see p. 269), since these simply postmodify the noun.

> Let's make sure the money goes to the people **who need it most**.
> The computer **(that) I borrowed** kept on crashing.

Separating items in a list

Commas are used to separate three or more items in a list or series.

> She got out bread, butter, and jam.
> You can stay here, come with us, or come later with Heather.

Note that the comma is often not placed before the final *and* or *or*.

> They breed dogs, cats, rabbits and hamsters.

Separating common expressions and their abbreviations

Commas are used to separate expressions in sentences that indicate to the reader what follows or could follow. These expressions include *for example*, *that is*, and *and so forth*, along with their common abbreviations: *e.g.*, *i.e.*, and *etc.*

> She got out bread, butter, jam, etc., and put them on the table.
> Several flavors are available, e.g., chocolate, caramel, strawberry,
>   and vanilla.
> His music is very accessible, i.e., easy to listen to.

Separating adjectives

Commas are used between adjectives, whether they come before the noun (i.e., used attributively) or after a linking verb (i.e., used predicatively).

> *It was a hot, dry, and dusty road.*
> *It's wet, cold, and windy outside.*

A comma is not usually used before an adjective that is followed by *and*.

With adverbials

When an adverbial such as *however*, *therefore* or *unfortunately* modifies a whole sentence, it is separated from the rest of the sentence by a comma.

> *However, police would not confirm this rumor.*
> *Therefore, I try to avoid using the car as much as possible.*

With sentence tags and short responses

Commas are used before sentence tags and after *yes* or *no* in short responses.

> *It's really cold today, isn't it?*
> *He's up to date with all his shots, isn't he?*
> *Are you the mother of these children? – Yes, I am.*
> *You're Amy Osborne, aren't you? – No, I'm not.*

With vocatives

Commas are used to separate the name of a person or group being addressed from the rest of the sentence.

> And now, ladies and gentlemen, please raise your glasses in
>   a toast to the happy couple.
> Come on, Olivia, be reasonable.
> Dad, can you come and help me, please?

With discourse markers

Commas are used to separate discourse markers like *Well* and *Now then* from the rest of the sentence.

> Well, believe it or not, I actually passed!
> Now then, let's see what's on TV tonight.
> Actually, I really enjoyed it.

In reported speech

Commas are used to follow direct speech (if there is no question or exclamation point after the quotation), or to show that it comes next.

> "I don't understand this question," said Peter.
> Peter said, "I don't understand this question."
> "You're crazy!" Claire exclaimed.
> "What do you think you're doing?" Dad bellowed.

It is also possible to punctuate reported speech of the type *Peter said*, "..." using a colon instead of a comma.

> Peter said: "Dream on."

In dates

A comma must be used between the day of the month and the year, when the two numbers are next to each other.

March 31, 2011

When a full date appears in a sentence it has both an internal comma and a comma after it.

As of March 31, 2011, your account will no longer be accessible via this website.

Quotation marks (" ") or (' ')

Direct speech

Direct speech gives the actual words that a speaker used. It is common in novels and other writing where the actual words of a speaker are quoted (see p. 277).

The words spoken are enclosed in double quotation marks.

> *"Have you been to the new shopping mall yet?" enquired Shona.*

> *"I've already seen it," John replied.*

- The comma comes inside the quotation marks.

Other uses

Double quotation marks are sometimes used:

– to suggest that the writer has some disagreement with use of the word or one of its meanings. These are informally called **scare quotes**.

> *I don't agree with this **"mercy killing"** business.*

– to indicate an unusual use of a word, or to show that a word you're using is new and not quite established.

> *She pointed out that the websites used for internet voting could be "spoofed."*

Single quotation marks are sometimes used:

– to draw attention to a word

> The word **'book'** can be used as a noun or a verb.
> There is no such word as **'fubber.'**
> Are there other acceptable spellings of **'kaballa'**?

– when one quotation is contained within another

> "I heard him say **'Wait for me'** but when I looked back he
> was gone," Lance said.

Capital letters

A capital (or upper case) letter is used to mark the beginning of a sentence.

> *When I was 20, I dropped out of college and became a model.*

Capital letters are also used for the first letter in proper nouns. These include:

– people's names

    Javon Forbes   *William Doudi*

– days of the week

    Wednesday   *Saturday*

– months of the year

    August   *January*

– public holidays

    Christmas   *Yom Kippur*

– nationalities

    Spanish   *Iraqi*

– languages

    Swahili   *Flemish*

– geographical locations

> *Arizona*   *Lake Powell*
> *Mount Everest*   *The Mediterranean Sea*

– company names

> *Dyson*   *HarperCollins*

– religions and systems of belief or thought

> *Islam*   *Buddhism*

Capital letters are also used for the first letter in titles of books, magazines, newspapers, TV shows, films, etc. Where there are several words, a capital letter is usually used for all the main content words in the title (i.e., not the prepositions or the determiners, unless they are the first word in the title).

> *The Times*   *Harper's*
> *Twelfth Night*   *The Secret Garden*
> *Newsnight*   *Mamma Mia!*

The period (.)

Periods are used:

– to mark the end of a sentence.

> *Let's have some lunch.*
> *I have to catch a bus in ten minutes.*

– to mark the end of a sentence fragment or sentence substitute.

> *Are you cold? – Yes, a bit.*
> *Do you like this sort of music? Not really.*

– in initials for people's names, although this practice is becoming less frequent.

> *J.K. Rowling*   *George W. Bush*
> *M.C. Hammer*   *Warren G. Harding*

– after some abbreviations, although this usage is variable and most abbreviations are clear without the period.

> *P.S. Do stop in next time you're passing through.*
> *She's moved to the I.T. department.*
> *R.S.V.P. to Helen Douglas on 555 2938.*
> *The U.S. government reacted strongly to the accusation.*

When an abbreviation consists of a shortened word such as *Soc.* or *Prof.*, a period is needed.

> *The Soc. of Retired Police Officers endorsed the decision.*
> *Prof. John Johansson will be speaking tonight.*
> *Flight UA 345: dep. 09:44 arr. 11:10.*

When an abbreviation contains the last letter of the shortened word, a period is also needed.

Dr. McDonald	*St. Mary's School*
41 Douglas Rd.	*the Akron Bar Assn.*

• Note that periods are not used in many common sets of initials,

> *Did you watch the game on NBC last night?*
> *Millions of people now call the FBI crimestopper line each year.*

or at the end of headlines, headings and titles.

> *Fear grips global stock markets*
> *Teaching grammar as a liberating force*
> *Wuthering Heights*

Remember that a period, and not a question mark, is used after an indirect question.

> *He asked if the bus had left.*
> *I wonder what's happened.*
> *She asked him where he was going.*

In British English, the period is called a full stop.

The question mark (?)

The question mark marks the end of a question.

> *When will we be arriving?*
> *Why did you do that?*
> *Does any of this matter?*
> *He's certain to be elected, isn't he?*

Question marks are used in direct questions, i.e., when the actual words of a speaker are used. A reported question should end with a period.

> *The lady said, "Where are you going?"*
> *The lady asked where she was going.*

Note that you put a question mark at the end of a question, even if the words in the sentence are not in the normal question order, or some words are omitted. Care is needed here as such a sentence can look, at first sight, like a statement rather than a question.

> *You know he doesn't live here any longer?*

A period, rather than a question mark, is used after an indirect question.

> *I'd like to know what you've been doing all this time.*
> *I wonder what's happened.*

The exclamation point (!)

The exclamation point (sometimes called the exclamation mark) is used after exclamations and emphatic expressions.

I can't believe it!
Oh, no! Look at this mess!

> The exclamation point loses its effect if it is overused. It is better to use a period after a sentence expressing mild excitement or humor.
>
> *It was such a beautiful day.*
> *I felt like a complete idiot.*

The colon (:)

The colon indicates a break between two main clauses that is stronger than a comma but weaker than a period.

A colon is used:

– in front of a list.

> *I used three colors: green, blue, and pink.*
> *Make sure you wear clothes made from natural fibers:*
>   *cotton, silk, or wool.*

– in front of an explanation or a reason.

> *Nevertheless, the main problem remained: what should*
>   *be done with the two men?*
> *I decided against going away this weekend: the weather*
>   *forecast was dreadful.*

– after introductory headings.

> *Cooking time: about five minutes.*
> *Start time: 10 o'clock.*

– to separate the hours from the minutes in expressions of time.

> *The conference call is scheduled for 10:45 this morning.*

– in more formal writing, between two main clauses that are connected.

> *It made me feel claustrophobic: what, I wonder, would happen*
>   *to someone who was really unable to tolerate being locked*
>   *into such a tiny space?*
> *Be patient: the next book in the series has not yet been*
>   *published.*

- in front of the second part of a book title.

> *Farming and Wildlife: a study in compromise*
> *Beyond Single Words: the most frequent collocations in spoken*
> *English.*

- to introduce direct speech, especially when the quotation is particularly long.

> *He said: "You owe me three dollars and twenty-five cents."*
> *The US Defense Secretary said: "There was agreement within*
> *the administration that we didn't think we were far enough*
> *down the road toward getting control of nuclear weapons*
> *around the world to limit ourselves so explicitly."*

The semicolon (;)

The semicolon is used to mark a break between two main clauses when there is a balance or a contrast between the clauses.

> Compare:
>
> *The engine roared into life. The propellers began to turn. The plane taxied down the runway ready for takeoff.*
>
> with:
>
> *The engine roared into life; the propellers began to turn; the plane taxied down the runway ready for takeoff.*

A useful test to decide when to use a semicolon is to ask yourself whether the two clauses could be written instead as separate sentences. If the answer is "yes", then you can use a semicolon.

Note that it is acceptable to use a period in these cases, but a semicolon is preferable if you wish to express a link or continuity between the clauses in your narrative.

> *I'm not that interested in jazz; I prefer classical music.*
> *He knew everything about me; I had never even heard of him.*

A semicolon is also used to separate items in a list, especially if the listed items are phrases or clauses that may already contain commas.

> *The trip was a disaster: the flight was four hours late; the hotel, which was described as "luxury," was dirty; and it rained for the whole week.*

Parentheses ( )

Parentheses are used to enclose a word or words that can be left out and still leave a meaningful sentence.

> *The wooded area (see map below) is approximately*
> *4,000 acres.*
> *This is a process which Hayek (a writer who came to*
> *rather different conclusions) also observed.*

Parentheses are also used to show alternatives or options.

> *Any student(s) interested in taking part should e-mail me.*
> *A goat should give from three to six pints (1.4 to 2.8 liters)*
> *of milk a day.*

Note that when the structure of the sentence as a whole requires punctuation after a section enclosed in parentheses, the punctuation is given *outside* the parentheses.

> *I haven't yet spoken to John (I mean John Maple, my boss),*
> *but I have a meeting with him on Friday.*
> *For lunch we had sandwiches (pastrami on rye and so on),*
> *salami, coleslaw, fried chicken, and potato salad.*

Punctuation is given before the closing parentheses only when it applies to the enclosed section rather than to the sentence as a whole.

> *He's very handsome (positively gorgeous in fact!) and still*
> *single.*

Brackets [ ]

Brackets (also called **square brackets**) are used, usually in books and articles, when supplying words that make a quotation clearer or that comment on it, although they were not originally said or written.

> *Mr. Runcie concluded: "The novel is at its strongest when describing the dignity of Cambridge [a slave] and the education of Emily [the daughter of an absentee landlord]."*

Brackets are also used when you need to put a word or word in parentheses inside another set of parentheses.

> *The novel touches on aspects of colonial life in India (the author, E.M. Forster [1879–1970], visited there in the 1920s).*

The hyphen (-)

The hyphen joins words or parts of words.

Hyphens are used at the ends of lines where a word has been split, to warn the reader that the word continues on the next line. If the word you need to split is clearly made up of two or more smaller words or elements, you should put the hyphen after the first of these parts. Otherwise, you put the hyphen at the end of a syllable. Most computer programs that deal with text insert hyphens automatically in acceptable places. Consult a dictionary if you are not sure where to insert the hyphen in a word.

> *wheelbar-row*　　　　　　*inter-national*
> *listen-ing*　　　　　　　*compli-mentary*
> *infor-mation*

It is best not to add a hyphen if the word is a short one, or if it would mean writing just one or two letters at the end or beginning of a line. For example, it would be better to write "unnatural" on the line below, rather than writing "un-" on one line and "natural" on the next.

Prefixes that are used in front of a word beginning with a capital letter always have a hyphen after them.

> *a wave of anti-Mexican feeling*
> *a neo-Byzantine cathedral*

A hyphen is used to join two or more words that together form an adjective, where this adjective is used *before* the noun it describes.

> *an up-to-date account*
> *a last-minute rush*
> *a six-year-old boy*

The hyphen is omitted when the adjective so formed comes after the noun or pronoun it describes.

> *The accounts are up to date.*
> *It was all rather last minute.*
> *He's six years old.*

Some common compound nouns are always written with hyphens.

> *mother-in-law*   *great-grandmother*

Hyphens can be used to split words that have been formed by adding a prefix to another word, especially to avoid an awkward combination of letters or confusion with another word.

> *co-owner*
> *re-covering furniture*
> *the re-creation of battle scenes*

Dashes

Printed books have two different kinds of dashes: the en dash (–) and the slightly longer em dash (—). These dashes can be created in most word-processing programs on computers, but in fact most people just use a hyphen where printed books use an en dash, and two hyphens (--) where printed books use an em dash. The information below applies mainly to the way dashes are used in printed books and professionally edited text.

The en dash (–)

An en dash is used:

– to indicate a range.

> *pages 26–42*

– between two adjectives or noun modifiers that indicate that two countries or groups are involved in something or that an individual has two roles or aspects.

> *Swedish–Norwegian relations improved*
> *the United States–Canada free trade pact*
> *a mathematician–philosopher*

– to indicate that something such as a plane or a train goes between two places.

> *the Anguilla–St. Kitts flight*
> *the New York–Montreal train*

The em dash (—)

An em dash is used:

- at the beginning and end of a comment that interrupts the flow of a sentence.

    Now children–Kenneth, stop that immediately!–open your books on page 20.

- to separate off extra information.

    Boots and shoes–all shapes, sizes and colors–tumbled out.

The slash (/)

The slash separates letters, words or numbers. It is used to indicate alternatives, ratios and ranges, and in website addresses. It is sometimes called a forward slash to distinguish it from a less frequently used character, the backslash (\).

> *he/she/it*
> *200 km/hr*
> *the 2011/12 accounting year*
> *http://www.abcdefg.com*

Punctuation in numbers

Dates

Slashes or periods are often used in dates.

	British usage
12/3/09	3.12.09
2/28/11	28.2.11

Abbreviations that indicate the era in which a date occurs are now usually written without periods after them, but periods are acceptable.

500 BCE   January 13, 1520 A.D.

Scientific usage

Periods are not used in metric system abbreviations.

12 kg   50 cm

Times

Colons are used in times. The letters *a.m.* and *p.m.* can be written with or without periods following them.

3:30 *a.m.*   20:30

Long numbers

Commas are used in numbers to mark off units of thousands, millions, billions, etc.

1,359   2,543,678

Decimals

Periods indicate decimal points.

1.5   25.08